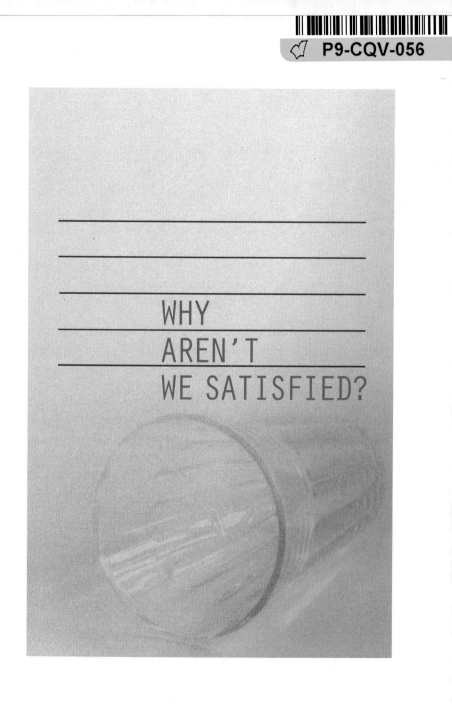

WHY
AREN'T
WE SATISFIED?

CLIFFORD WILLIAMS

WITH ALL
THAT WE
HAVE
WHY
AREN'T
WE SATISFIED?

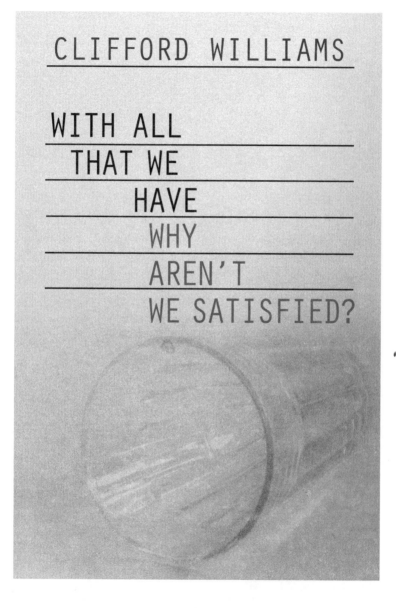

 SORIN BOOKS Notre Dame, IN

Scripture quotations are from the *New Revised Standard Version* of the Bible, copyright © 1993 and 1989 by the Division of Christian Education of the National Council of Churches of Christ in the U.S.A. Used by permission. All rights reserved.

International Standard Book Number: 1-893732-23-1

Cover design by Eric Walljasper

Text design by Katherine Robinson Coleman

Printed and bound in the United States of America.

Library of Congress Cataloging-in-Publication Data
Williams, Clifford, 1943-
With all that we have-- why aren't we satisfied? / Clifford Williams.
     p. cm.
     Includes bibliographical references (p.   ).
     ISBN 1-893732-23-1
     1. Spiritual life--Christianity. I. Title.
BV4501.3 .W55 2001
248.4--dc21   00-011330
                                                 CIP

CONTENTS

ACKNOWLEDGMENTS

The meditations in this book are based on weekly meditations I have been giving in my classes at Trinity College since 1984. I thank all who have listened to them, Janel Rowland for suggesting I make a book out of them, and Trinity College for providing a context in which to create them.

Two of the meditations have been published before in slightly altered form. They are, "God's Clowns," *The Evangelical Beacon* (February 1, 1983), p. 14; "Vulnerable People—Victims Forever?" *The Marian Helpers Bulletin* (October-December, 1984), p. 21. Used with permission. The poem by Sister Maura Eichner, "Bethlehem," appeared in *Walking on Water* (Newman Press, 1972), and is used with permission of the author.

Most of us feel a nagging emptiness, like something is missing from our lives. There is more we could be taking in or giving out and more we could be experiencing. Even after an exhilarating moment, we experience a letdown. On occasion, the emptiness feels like a craving or even a desperation.

Sometimes we think we know what it would take to dispel the hollowness within. If we had more adventure or excitement, we think, it would vanish. Or if we had a love that brought grand surprises, the gnawing discontent would go away. Maybe some new friend or a respected achievement would do the same, or a purchase or a change of jobs.

Other times we are not sure what would make us content. On these occasions, we feel a vague dissatisfaction tinged with an aggravating boredom. We do not know what we are looking for and are not sure we would recognize it if we were to encounter it.

Too often we try to fill our emptiness in ways that do not work. We pile up possessions and successes instead of attending to the hurts of acquaintances or noticing their moral beauty. We substitute trivial projects for significant ones, chase cheap thrills instead of seeking lasting delights.

There are times, too, when we simply close down, preferring the pain of emptiness. We keep others at bay rather than connect with them. We live in narrow and constricted ways instead of loving extravagantly.

The obvious question is, Why not give up the artificial means we use to try to dissolve our restless emptiness? Why not open up and go for the only thing that works—God?

One wants to think of this last question as rhetorical. However, there are deep forces within us that make it a real

question. We are addicted to envy and pride; we passionately
want to be known as superior to others; we are broken by
tragedies we can scarcely acknowledge, from which we do
not seem to be able to break free. If we are going to be fully
content, we are going to have to root out these addictions
and passions.

Why Aren't We Satisfied? describes some of these deep
forces. It also describes some of the prominent features of
what a truly contented life would look like. Each meditation is like a bulging suitcase—once you open it, the contents spill out. Suitcases, of course, are meant to be opened
and their contents are meant to be taken out and used. But
if you have a lot in your suitcase, you will have a lot to deal
with when you open it.

It is best, accordingly, to read no more than several of
these meditations at a time. The aphorisms at the end of the
meditations are succinct sayings that overflow in a number
of different directions, likewise to be encountered only a
few at a time.

I remind the reader that the author has his own share of
emptiness. He, too, tries to fill it in ways that do not work
and sometimes closes down. These meditations are as
much *for* him as they are *by* him.

ONE

DRIED-UP HUMAN HEARTS

The meditations in this first section focus on our ground-level desires. These are the ones that remain after we have stripped away our everyday desires. They also produce our everyday desires, which are products of the ground-level desires. Consider, for instance, our craving for adventure. It is not itself a rock-bottom desire, derived from nothing larger in human nature. It is, rather, an outgrowth of our need for an overall direction. The same is true of our desire for newness. It, too, comes from our need to find a direction worth adopting.

The disconcerting fact about these ground-level desires is that they seem never to be fully satisfied. Some of them, some of the time, seem not to be satisfied at all. If they were fully satisfied, we would never be restless or discontented. But we are restless and we are discontented. Would we crave adventure or newness if we were not?

Adventures can, of course, be the outgrowth of a fulfilled heart, and newness can be a manifestation of our love for God. More often, though, they are ways of trying to satisfy unfulfilled spiritual hunger.

The first step to a larger spiritual life is to become aware of our ground-level desires. It is to say to ourselves, "Yes, I really do want a higher kind of delight. I do sometimes dream of love." In different words, it is to become aware of our desire to satisfy genuine spiritual hunger. It is to say, "My heart is cold and needs to be warm, dried-up and needs to be brought to life again."

HUNGER FOR GOD

The writer of Psalm 42 says that he longs for God in the same way a thirsty deer longs for a stream of cool water.

The first thing to notice about the Psalmist's experience is that it is representative of our own. We, too, hunger and thirst for God. We also hunger for love and community. To hunger for these means that we feel a need for them. We feel that something is lacking in us, something is missing that we perceive we need. Truly to hunger for them is to feel this lack intensely.

Another point to notice is that sometimes we are aware of this hunger, sometimes we are not, and sometimes we squash it. In the first of these, we feel the hunger, know that we lack something, and are drawn toward love, community, and God. We are conscious of the fact that we want these.

In the second, we do not feel the hunger. It may be that we are so preoccupied with other matters that we do not notice our hunger, or it may be that we have become so immersed in routine that we become numb. In any case, it is possible for us to be unaware or only vaguely aware that we want love, community, and God.

In the third case, even though we notice our hunger, we push it away. We may do so because we fear what would happen if we had love, community, or God in our lives. Or we want something different, such as admiration, success, or money. As a result, we remain hungry and empty.

The significant fact about our hunger for love, community, and God is that it can push us toward them. In fact, our hunger for these may be a more powerful motivator than duty.

It is tragic to go through life with unfulfilled hunger. It is tragic to be continually numb to our hunger, continually to deny our need for love, community, and God, and constantly to squash the very thing that would lead us to God if we would let it.

Perhaps part of becoming more spiritually alive is becoming aware of our hunger for God, and perhaps part of maturing in faith is staying aware of it, not squashing it, crowding it out, or becoming numb.

> The one who is most filled with God is also most hungry for God.

DRIED-UP HUMAN HEARTS

In Honore de Balzac's novel *Pere Goriot*, the narrator asks at one point, "Who shall say which is more ghastly, the sight of bleached skulls or of dried-up human hearts?"

Having a dried-up heart is, indeed, ghastly to think about. The sense of tragedy we feel when we contemplate such a possibility exceeds by far the revulsion, bleakness, and sadness we would feel upon encountering a field full of human skulls, bleached white by the beating sun.

What is a dried-up human heart? It is one that is not vibrant or pulsating. It is numb and does not feel. It is not affected by others' plights. It is not able to give, because it has nothing to give. It is shriveled up, sunk in on itself. It is inert, passive, and does nothing.

In contrast, a human heart that is not dried-up is vibrant and pulsating. It feels, is soft, and is affected by the suffering of others. It is able to give, because it is overflowing. It is expansive and active.

Although we react negatively to the thought of a dried-up human heart, there is something in us that is afraid of letting our hearts become vibrant and soft and giving and expansive. These are new, and we hang on to the old. We like our numbness and do not want it to be replaced. We cling to our hardness and insulate ourselves from the suffering of others. We allow our hearts to be shriveled and bleached.

One remedy for such an unappetizing state is to allow ourselves to be loved. Love softens hardness; it expands shriveled-up things and makes numb things feel.

One way to allow ourselves to be loved is to picture ourselves being loved: to imagine ourselves being held in large, loving hands; to think of ourselves as chicks who are covered by the wings of their mother; to picture the smiling face of one who has kind eyes looking at us with rapt delight.

To feel fright at the thought of a dried-up heart is to begin to enliven it.

OUR DEEPEST NEEDS

We often drift though life without asking ourselves what our deepest needs are. When we do ask and are honest with the answer, we come face to face with our true condition, which can be rather unsettling. It can, however, prod us to seek faith.

One need is for inner peace. All of us experience inner turmoil at times—anxiety, loneliness, fear, despair, confusion, doubt, and insecurity. Faith gives us an inner serenity that helps dispel this turmoil. Although we constantly struggle with these feelings, faith's presence helps squeeze out inner unrest.

A second need is to be forgiven. All of us have felt guilty. It is a painful feeling, perhaps the most painful feeling we have in life. We cannot live with ourselves if we let this feeling continue for very long. The forgiveness that comes from faith though, frees us and enables us to live with ourselves.

A third need is to be loved. The truth is that, more often than we would like to admit, we do not feel loved. This fact impels us to seek acceptance in a variety of ways—in success, wealth, clothes, education, wit, job performance, and more, much more. Though we may find it hard to have faith in God's acceptance of us, when we do, we sense deeply that we are loved.

A fourth need is to be with someone, to be in community. In an important sense, all of us are alone. We must find meaning for our lives; no one else can find it for us. We ourselves must deal with guilt; no one else can do that for us. We ourselves must die; no one else can die in our place. Even though we have friends, and even though we assuage our loneliness by being with them, we still are alone. But faith overcomes that aloneness. Faith gives us community at a basic level, because we are connecting to Someone who is always there. We do not have to deal with meaning, guilt, and death alone.

A fifth need is for meaning in our lives. Without meaning we would lose hope and feel that our lives are futile. So strong is our need for meaning that we strive to find it in a myriad of ways, many of them unsatisfactory. Faith is pertinent to our constant search for something that makes our lives worthwhile. It disperses the futility we might feel when we ask ourselves what we are doing with our lives.

A sixth need is to live beyond death. The inescapable fact about human existence is that we die. Because we dread death, we avoid thinking about it or we tell ourselves that we are not going to die. It happens to other people but not to us, we convince ourselves. Faith gives us the ability to face death. No longer do we have to deny it, though we are still tempted to do so, and no longer do we have to bear its sting alone, though we still feel as if we do.

Often we are not aware that these are our needs. Nevertheless, they are the driving forces of our lives. We need to be conscious of this fact, and internalize the truth that only faith genuinely satisfies.

What we need most is a passion to work on fulfilling our basic needs.

SPIRITUAL HUNGER

There are times in everyone's life when boredom sets in. It may be boredom with something specific, such as a job, the house in which we live, or a meeting. It may be boredom with something less specific, such as living spiritually or even life in general. Boredom with something specific can be relatively easy to remedy—we can simply do something else. Boredom with life in general is not so easily remedied.

Blaise Pascal suggests that the remedy for spiritual boredom is spiritual hunger. "We do not grow bored," he writes, "with eating and sleeping every day, for we soon feel hungry or sleepy again; otherwise we should grow bored with it. Likewise if we do not hunger for spiritual things we find them boring."[1]

Like physical hunger, spiritual hunger is a craving, a desire, an irresistible impulse. It is a passion, an intense interest. The Psalmist describes it as a longing: "As a deer longs for a stream of cool water, so I long for you, O God."[2]

Pascal described the objects of spiritual hunger as "spiritual things." These might include knowing God, loving people, and knowing ourselves. One of the beatitudes in the Sermon on the Mount uses the word "righteousness" to describe the object of our hunger.

If we are hungry for knowing God, we will find ourselves craving that knowledge if we go without it for a period of time, just as we crave food when we go without it for too long. If we are hungry for loving people, our drive to love will increase in intensity the longer it remains unsatisfied.

What we will discover as we develop these hungers is that they squeeze out boredom. The hunger itself does this, and so also does the satisfaction of the hunger.

How can we get this spiritual hunger? Can we just make ourselves have it? Can we simply choose it? Do we have to wait until it comes over us? Can we give it to ourselves or must we get it from God? Can we ask God to give it to us without already having some?

The answers to these questions are not obvious, but what does seem certain is that spiritual hunger is central to living a larger spiritual life. Without it we will become jaded, mechanically acting in the ways we think others think we should act. With it, we will experience some of the most intense delights imaginable.

If we felt whole-life boredom more often, we might feel spiritual hunger more often as well.

DESIRING HUMILITY

In his spiritual autobiography, Frederick Suppe, a philosopher of science, writes, "I want, I desperately seek, humility." What he wanted was not to demean himself but to excise the false show that he was constantly tempted to put on.

When we take an inventory of our desires, we find that we have numerous ones that crowd out the desire for humility. These include everyday desires, desires to achieve specific goals, and whole-life desires. There are so many of these other kinds of desires that the desire for humility gets pushed out.

We also have within us a conflicting desire, namely, the desire to appear "bigger" than we actually are, the desire to flaunt our accomplishments, possessions, or good qualities, so that others will take notice and admire us. So the desire for humility also gets pushed out by our active opposition to it.

We can, however, cultivate the desire for humility. We can become aware of the presence of our other desires and the absence of a desire for humility. We can become aware of the desire to flaunt. We can focus our attention on the attractiveness of humility and let its goodness draw us to it. Doing this will cause the other desires to recede in importance and will induce the desire to flaunt to lose its grip on us.

Having said these things, I want to observe that obtaining humility may not in the end be as much a matter of desiring it as a matter of allowing ourselves to be loved. Humility may come more from soaking in God's love than from deliberate desire. If this is so, we would not possess humility because we consciously seek it but because the love in us brings it about. The key, then, would be to allow God's love into our lives more and more.

Part of us desires humility, but part of us nurtures unwarranted pride.

THE WORST SIN

Some segments of our culture regard abortion, homosexuality, and other taboos as the worst sins. Other segments have a different list of worst sins.

There is, I believe, a sin that is worse than any popularly denounced sin. It is indifference.

Indifference is a neglected sin, hardly ever the subject of an essay or sermon. Yet it kills the spiritual life more surely than any public transgression.

The essence of indifference is spiritual laziness. Its opposites are interest, desire, and driving force.

Although indifference's opposites often result in our becoming active, spiritual energy should not be identified with such activity. Our activities often are simply the product of a desire to escape boredom, or they come from a vague impulse to ward off spiritual emptiness. The opposite of indifference is caring about spiritual matters. It is a passion in our heart's core.

The presence of indifference does a number of things. It undermines compassion, blinds us to our expansive egos, diminishes interest in victims of economic oppression, makes us unable to see distress in another's face, produces disinterest in peacemaking activities, makes us merely go through the motions of being spiritual, causes us to sit listlessly in front of our televisions for hours each week, makes love for God diminish, and blinds us to opportunities to love. In general, it de-energizes us so that even if we notice opportunities for compassion we remain motionless on our couches. Indifference causes us to be unmotivated to pursue a larger life. In short, it brings about a living death.

> Little is worse than going through our whole lives indifferent and dead.

OUR NEED FOR FAITH, HOPE, AND LOVE

We often conceive of faith, hope, and love as conditions we are supposed to possess or as ideals we should try to exemplify. They are these, to be sure, but they are also deep longings.

To become aware that we have intense needs for faith, hope, and love, we need only ask ourselves what it would be like not to have them. With faith, we have something to trust in: What would life be like if we could not trust anything? With hope, we have something to look forward to: What would our lives be like if there were nothing we could look forward to? With love, we have something to give ourselves to: What would it be like if there were no one we could give ourselves to? With love, too, we allow ourselves to be loved: What would it be like if we never let anyone love us?

We need faith, hope, and love, and without them we would be empty. Perhaps one approach to pursuing a larger life is to view it as a process of awakening the awareness of our need for these, working at intensifying our desire for them, then letting these desires gently push us.

> We come alive only when we become aware
> of our deepest longings.

DEEP PAIN AT NOT HAVING LOVED
AS WE HAVE BEEN LOVED

In one of his discourses, Søren Kierkegaard wrote, "Did you keep the apostolic words holy? Did you treasure them in a pure and beautiful heart and refuse to be ransomed . . . from the deep pain of having to confess again and again that you never loved as you were loved?"[3]

Most of the pain we have is unwanted. This is certainly true for emotional pain, such as that resulting from a loss of some sort or from criticism, low self-esteem, a breakup with a boyfriend or girlfriend, or uncertainty about the future. It is also true that most moral and spiritual pains are unwanted. Remorse, envy, and bitterness at an injustice done to us are pains we want gone.

There is another kind of pain, though, that is good to have: the deep pain of realizing that we have not loved as we have been loved. For this pain is a call from eternity. It is sorrow that our lives have not been as they might have been. It springs from reflection on how we can love as we have been loved. It pushes us toward that love and incites us to confession and repentance. It is an awakening to something new in our lives. It makes us see ourselves as being loved by the one whose love has no bounds.

Here is a pain worth having, a pain worth feeling from time to time, a pain worth experiencing deeply.

> Some pains make us want to pity ourselves,
> others to flee ourselves, and still others
> to remake ourselves.

SPIRITUAL DELIGHT

Imagine a child who is opening a gift. She has an excited anticipation as she tears off the wrapping paper. Upon first seeing the gift itself, she is awe-struck. A bright smile displays itself on her face, and perhaps she gives in to the impulse to twirl and jump with glee. We have here an instance of skip-and-dance delight.

There is a calmer kind of delight that consists of a quiet and more lasting exhilaration. This second kind of delight spreads through us with a certain warmth. Perhaps we can call it warmhearted delight.

Too often, however, both of these kinds of delight get squeezed out by an inner propensity toward paleness. Something in us is uncomfortable with delight; sometimes, even, we are positively afraid of it. It is as if we cannot open the gift of love. We hold it in our hands with a studied indifference or with an unconscious unconcern.

Delight gets squeezed out as well by our proclivity toward darkness. We prefer to notice the faults in others instead of their good features. It is much easier to criticize than to praise. We would rather be glum than happy. These tendencies produce feelings in us that are the opposite of delight.

Delight also gets set aside by routine activities, which often bring about a dullness to which we become addicted. In addition, delight must see past the anger, resentment, bitterness, disappointment, annoyance, and other emotions that inevitably arise from time to time.

So delight is not easy to come by. To possess it we must root out indifference, dark impulses, envy, and boredom. We have to let new desires grow in us so that we come more and more to take pleasure in goodness and love. We must, in short, become different kinds of persons.

This delight is one feature of a larger and more expansive life. This life is not constricted by pale emotions or destructive impulses, and it possesses some of the same keen enjoyment in loving that God possesses.

What would it be like if we thought of love as a gift? What would it be like if we thought of friendship as a gift, of contacts with people as gifts, of God's love as a gift, and, indeed, of life itself as a gift, each of which we could open with spontaneous delight and warmhearted exuberance?

Delight is the spark that sets our hearts ablaze.

SORROW AS AN ELEMENT OF REPENTANCE

Webster's Dictionary defines sorrow as "deep distress and regret as over the loss of something loved, a display of grief or sadness."

The occasions when we normally experience grief and sadness are at the death of a friend or relative and times when we learn of people who have been victims of catastrophes, abuse, or misfortune. Sometimes we have sorrow for those who are wasting their lives, wandering aimlessly, or falling into traps of their own making. We are sad when someone we know becomes ill, gets a divorce, or cannot bear painful memories.

Our lives are tragedies, too, for something has not been right between us and the one who made us. We often try to rectify this condition in a myriad of ways that do not work. We have fled God and ignored him.

When we feel sorrow at the tragedy of our lives, we are ready to admit that we need God. This sorrow does not come easily, nor is it a one-time affair at the beginning of our spiritual journey. It is a continuing feature of it.

> The hardest but most fitting sorrow is for the messes of our own making.

DAYDREAMS

Without daydreams, life would be as tasteless as potatoes without salt. Daydreams give us refuge from the painful realities of a harsh world. They provide us with experiences we cannot have in real life. In our daydreams we relax in the midst of burdensome tasks. We travel to exciting places and lie on warm beaches in the middle of chilling winters.

Daydreams also reveal who we are. If we envision ourselves receiving standing ovations because of our great performances, that says one thing. If we imagine ourselves being chased by angry people, that says something else.

One revealing characteristic of our daydreams is that their protagonist is nearly always ourselves. We dream about what *we* want to do, the good times *we* can have, the exciting adventures in which *we* can engage. It is *our* projects, *our* hopes for the future, and *our* circumstances about which we dream.

No doubt it gives us great pleasure to dream about ourselves. Daydreams are a salve for life's wounds. And no doubt it is necessary to have a certain amount of this salve in order for life to be bearable.

Yet there is a nagging question: Why do our daydreams involve just ourselves and our interests? Why cannot some of them include other people's interests? Why, for example, can we not dream about the contentment our acquaintances would have if they were to allow themselves to be loved, or about the sense of respect unemployed people would have if they were employed, or about the calm exhilaration people would experience if they were to take in more beauty and goodness?

When a person has been prevented from doing something she especially likes to do, she pictures herself doing it every now and then. Occasionally, she will imagine herself riding her bicycle on country roads, or being with a certain person, or going to a certain place.

When a person delights in God's ways, she, too, thinks about concerns that exhibit these ways. Some of her reveries will be about people who exemplify wisdom and self-control. Others will be about circumstances that display love to the helpless. Still others, perhaps, will be about transformed friends.

What would the world be like, what would we be like, if we had daydreams of giving-love?

> You can tell what a person is really like by knowing what she daydreams about.

TWO

FALLING IN LOVE WITH
THE IDEA OF LOVE

There are two processes by which our faith can wither. The first is to succumb to attacks from alien values. The thought patterns of a culture that is hostile to genuine spirituality seep into our mind. Behavior that we once regarded as unacceptable we come to regard as not so bad after all. We give up trying to fight the enemy and let the ways of the world become our own.

The second process involves the faith group of which we are a part. Group pressure to exemplify certain virtues causes us to pretend to be virtuous. Frequent talk of love makes us love the idea of love more than love itself. Insulating ourselves from different groups causes us to regard others as inferior and ourselves as superior. Awareness of our need for forgiveness decreases as the desire to maintain a positive image in the group increases. In the end, our faith becomes artificial, which is to say that it has disappeared.

This second process, though it is as effective in destroying faith as the first, is much less recognized than the first. It operates more at the unconscious level. Those who succumb to it vehemently assert the reality of their faith. What is needed, therefore, is awareness—awareness of our impulse to pretend, of our drive to think of ourselves as being better than others, and last, of our need to be forgiven.

WHO IS THE ENEMY?

A common complaint about secular society is that there is too much crime, too much secularism in the schools, not enough people who are willing to get involved, or too many people who don't care about violence. In religious communities, the complaint might be that there is too much superficiality, not enough people who encourage others, or too many who just go through the motions of being good.

These complaints no doubt are true, and we need for them to be said. We need astute social analysis from a spiritual and moral perspective and we need perceptive insights into life in a community of faith. There certainly are a variety of sins that need to be stamped out.

Yet there is a temptation: to focus so much on the sins of others or on the sin of the "impersonal other" that we forget our own need to work on spirituality. This is, indeed, a delicious temptation. *They* need to have the right values, *they* need to know God, *they* need to live a deeper and more meaningful life, *they* need to escape superficiality. Thinking these things becomes a perfect dodge to run from our own spiritual state, a dodge that we find nearly irresistible. It is not falsity that tempts here, but truth.

The truth is that *we* need to love better, *we* need to become better encouragers, *we* need God's mercy. The correct attitude is, in a way, to forget about the failings of others and focus on ourselves. The picture we need to have is of the tax collector who prayed, "God, be merciful to me, a sinner." He was not pointing his finger at other sinners, but humbly seeking mercy for his own sinfulness.

Who is the enemy? It is, to be sure, people who cause trouble and do violence, lukewarm believers, and the like. But it is also us. Pogo once exclaimed in a memorable comic strip, "We have met the enemy, and he is us."

It is more tempting to think more that others need to change than that we need to change.

RELIGIOUS PRETENDING

In "Please Hear What I'm Not Saying," Charles Finn writes,

> I panic at the thought of my weakness and fear
> being exposed.
> That's why I frantically create a mask to hide
> behind,
> a nonchalant sophisticated facade,
> to help me pretend,
> to shield me from the glance that knows.

There are many everyday ways of pretending, and there are religious ways of pretending. We are afraid of what others will think of us, so we pretend to be good. We pretend to be perfect in every way, people who are never tempted, never struggle with doubt, and are always joyful. Who of us would dare admit that sometimes we do not feel like being good or spiritual, that we have unmentionable dreams, that we do not know whether we really believe, that we are hardly ever joyful (even though we smile profusely), or that we like being proud? The fear of what others would say or think is too intense and the pressure of conformity is too strong to allow us to confess these. So we create masks to hide behind.

These masks can operate not only with everyday struggles, but also with more cosmic ones. We may have worn the mask, "I am good" or "I am a Christian," all our lives, even though we are not. Pretending occurs both with respect to painful emotions and with respect to our basic self-concepts.

What is the remedy for pretending? Certainly a fair amount of courage is needed to take off our masks. In addition, if you indicated to me in words, body language, and facial expression that you take me as I am, I might feel your acceptance and remove my masks. I might feel God's love more intensely and more frequently than I now do. Likewise, if I indicated to you that I take you as you are, you might feel acceptance and remove your masks. You might feel God's love more deeply as well.

If we had the same stance toward others that we want them to have toward us, they would take their masks off.

ARTIFICIAL CHRISTIANITY IN CHRISTIAN GROUPS

By artificial Christianity I mean two things: (1) going through the motions of the Christian life without really being a Christian, and (2) thinking that one is a Christian because one goes through the motions, even though one knows at some level that the motions do not make one a Christian.

There are several features of churches and other Christian groups that make being an artificial Christian easy. The first is that there is pressure to be smiling and happy. A Christian group expects its members to be good Christians. The result is that many in the group are led to pretend. They exhibit smiling faces, say the right things, and act in accepted ways, but on the inside may be numb, turbulent, or empty.

A second feature is that, like all groups, Christian groups exert pressure on their members to conform. In succumbing to this pressure, the members of the group identify with it, imagining that they have the characteristics that the group has. The result is that they "live outside themselves." The Christianity they imagine themselves possessing is really the group's; they have become crowd Christians even though they are aware that being one is not what makes one a real Christian. The sense of conformity to the group has replaced the experience of sorrow in contrition and of newness in grace.

A third feature of Christian groups is that in them there does not appear to be any enemy. A church is not like secular culture, where drinking, drugs, sex, and parties take place much more frequently. There is no explicit antagonism to Christianity in a Christian group. As a result, those in Christian groups tend to let their Christianity become easy. They forget that self-justification eats away at faith, that envy undermines grace, that self-admiration creeps into their thinking, that comparison expands egos, that indifference undercuts love, that busyness numbs, and that resistance to goodness rumbles around in the core of one's personality.

The consequence of these features of Christian groups is that Christian activities become a way of running from God. The very things that Christians think are expressions of Christianity are methods of resisting Christianity.

How can one cut through this artificiality? One thing that can be done is to put one's Bible in the back corner of a drawer for a couple of weeks, and find a quiet place and sit for an hour or two, listening to God. Another thing to do is to tune out what is going on during a church service and pray the tax collector's prayer ("God, be merciful to me, a sinner") the whole time.

Artificial faith often looks like real faith.

THE OFFICIAL LIE

By the official lie I mean that we act as if everything is okay even though it is not. The lie is exhibited in smiling faces, in doing the things expected of one in a community of faith, such as saying proper prayers in public, paying attention in church, and in general being cheery.

The truth is that not everything is okay. We struggle with our faith, we are tempted and sometimes give in, on occasion we do not feel like being good, we doubt our worth, and we have painful and disrupting memories.

Why is the official lie perpetuated? Perhaps the principal reason is the pressure to be like others. It is nearly impossible to overestimate this pressure. Whenever two or three are together, it begins to operate. Sometimes it is quite explicit, especially in groups in which there are definite expectations about how one should live. Often, though, it is mostly implicit. It consists of the unspoken assumption that it is not proper to display signs of spiritual weakness.

Because of our fear of how other people would react if we were to admit our weaknesses, we become afraid to admit the truth about ourselves. Often the reactions of others confirm our fears, so we shut up and pretend that things are just fine.

What happens next is that we begin to believe the lie. We come to think of ourselves as good people who are living as God wishes, as ones who fit in well with our community of faith, unlike others who aren't quite there yet or who are definitely on the outside.

My plea is for us to be honest. My plea is also for us to be accepting of other people's honesty, for without such acceptance, they will start lying to us, for the same reason we have lied to them.

The official lie is a silent conspiracy into which we fall with little conscious thought—or resistance.

FALLING IN LOVE WITH THE IDEA OF LOVE

The idea of love is a marvelous idea. When we think of how wonderful the world would be with more love, we cannot help becoming enthralled. When we imagine how people's lives would be transformed if only they knew love, we behold with awe its power to make people new.

As wonderful as the idea of love is, it is, nevertheless, merely an idea. The idea of love does not hurt, but real love does, for real love identifies with the hurts of others. The idea of love does not change lives, but real love does. The idea of love does not give, but real love does.

The idea of faith, too, is a marvelous idea. It is the idea of something that enables people to live in new and wonderful ways. As important as the idea of faith is, though, it is just an idea. The idea of faith is not delight in spiritual things, but real faith is.

The ideas of sin and grace are significant ideas, too. The idea of sin makes sense of human experience, and the idea of grace gives us a way of dealing with sin. These ideas remain mere ideas, however, until we feel the sorrow of doing wrong and experience the forgiveness in grace.

It is easy to fall in love with the idea of love. It is, after all, a marvelous idea. And it is just as easy to fall in love with the ideas of faith and grace, for these, too, are attractive ideas.

Moreover, and here is the rub, it is easy to mistake the idea of love for the real thing. It is easy to identify the ideas of faith and grace with real faith and grace. All that we have to do is imagine that we love and that we have faith. The truth is, though, that the ideas are not the real thing. The real thing is far different and much more wonderful.

> The idea of a rich and active life often feels as pleasing as the life itself.

THE TAX COLLECTOR AND THE PHARISEE:

WHO IS THE HERO?

One of the most pivotal stories Jesus told was the story of the Pharisee and the tax collector:

> Two men went up to the temple to pray, one a Pharisee and the other a tax collector. The Pharisee, standing by himself, was praying thus, "God, I thank you that I am not like other people: thieves, rogues, adulterers, or even like this tax collector. I fast twice a week; I give a tenth of all my income." But the tax collector, standing far off, would not even look up to heaven, but was beating his breast and saying, "God, be merciful to me, a sinner." I tell you, this man went down to his home justified rather than the other (Luke 18:10-14).

When we ask, "Would the Pharisee or the tax collector be more welcome in a church?" the obvious answer is that the Pharisee would. He did all the right things, refrained from all the wrong things, no doubt was well-dressed, and was known for his piety. The tax collector cheated, extorted, skimmed money off the top of the tax he collected, and had a shady reputation. Yet the tax collector is presented by Jesus as the hero of the story. Why is this so?

In the first place, the tax collector was willing to admit his cheating, whereas the Pharisee was not willing to admit his shortcomings. The tax collector knew that something was not right with his life, but the Pharisee was well satisfied with his religious life.

In the second place, the tax collector did not use his good features (he surely was not all bad) to justify himself, whereas the Pharisee did. Notice, though, that the Pharisee's self-justification, though explicit in the story, was not his public posture. (Who could have tolerated his "I am good because I tithe"?) Publicly, he displayed contriteness, perhaps even reading the forgiveness Psalms at worship services. The tax collector, however, did not display his contriteness publicly, partly because he was not allowed to be at worship services, and partly out of fear that self-justification might creep in by such a display.

Third, the tax collector saw God's forgiving love as the source of his rightness, whereas the Pharisee used comparison to found his rightness. The Pharisee knew, rightly, that he was different from others, and the knowledge of this difference dominated his consciousness. Like the Pharisee, the tax collector could have boasted about something in himself that was superior to others, maybe even superior to the Pharisee, but he did not. Rather, he let his consciousness be dominated by mercy.

The tax collector is the hero of Jesus' story because he did not succumb to the Pharisee's self-justification. Perhaps, though, we should not *think* of him as the hero, for once we do, we identify with him and think of ourselves as

superior to the Pharisee, who did succumb to his impulses
of self-justification. In doing so, we fall back into self-
justification. By identifying instead with the story's anti-
hero, the Pharisee, we become like the hero.

There is a bit of Pharisee and tax collector in
everyone who aspires to genuine faith.

THE GENUINE BELIEVER

There are two ways we can think about the genuine
believer. First, we can think of her as one who is loving and
gentle, has firm convictions, is not consumed by envy or
conceit, has self-control, prays, is an encourager and a
peacemaker, keeps promises, is faithful to a spouse if married, is celibate if not, listens to others' feelings, uses gracious words, does not have any addictions, and in sum is
one whose life is a witness to the divine.

There is, however, a danger in thinking of the genuine
believer only in this first way, by focusing our attention on
the good qualities of the believer, we forget the honesty and
confessional aspects of being a believer.

In the second concept of the genuine believer, we think
of her as one who admits to falling short in many ways. She
thinks of herself as not as loving as she really wants to be,
as giving in to envy too often, as missing opportunities to

encourage or promote peace. She confesses these short-comings to herself, to God, and sometimes to others.

The first concept, without the second, is more like the good religious person about whom Jesus had so many negative things to say. The second concept is more like the tax collector, who was too honest to fit in and who had to stand across the street from the temple to pray, "God, be merciful to me, one who lusts and is envious and lazy and cares more about my own pet projects than others' distress."

Self-honesty comes hard to those who regard themselves as decent people worthy of being admired.

THE IDEAL CHURCH

The parable of the prodigal son raises an intriguing question about what an ideal church should be.

> There was a man who had two sons. . . . The younger son gathered all he had and traveled to a distant country, and there he squandered his property in dissolute living. . . . When he came to himself . . . he went to his father. But while he was still far off, his father saw him and was filled with compassion; he ran and put his arms around him and kissed him (Luke 15:11-24).

An attractive picture of the ideal church is of a church in which people are friendly and accepting, there is concern for those outside the church, members are active in worthy pursuits, harmony is prevalent, there is a lively interest in discovering the ways of God, and in general, members live exemplary and virtuous lives. Although this description of an ideal church is appealing, the parable of the prodigal son makes one wonder whether something in it is missing. The prodigal son had none of the characteristics of a member of an ideal church. He partied and spent his money on prostitutes; perhaps he gambled as well and consorted with rough or sleazy looking people; no doubt he used street language. Yet he was accepted by his father in spite of this. If we take the story of the prodigal son as a paradigm of how we should respond to those who have been wayward, then we should think of churches as being welcoming to gamblers, prostitutes, drug addicts, thieves, bar hoppers, and gang members.

In a church that is not welcoming to prodigal son types, there is likely to be an atmosphere in which it is assumed that members are good and upright and that outsiders are not. "We" are acceptable and "they" are not, it is felt. This mentality obscures the truth that church people have cheated, have sported with sex, and have been unjustly critical of others. It neatly hides the fact that if their inner lives were open to public inspection, they would shrink in terror and shame. In a church of prodigals, however, the attitude toward outsiders would not be, "You are bad but I am not." Instead, it would be, "Each of us is a sinner in need of forgiveness."

Moreover, in a church where everyone is fine and upstanding, an atmosphere is fostered in which people accept others in the church because they are good. Their demonstrated character and reputation for saying and doing the right things are the basis of their acceptability. In a church of prodigals, by contrast, the atmosphere is one in which members are acceptable "just because." It is not public demonstration of good character that is paramount, but an open display of the attitude, "I take you the way you are."

In addition, in a church where people think of themselves as good and virtuous, there is likely to be the feeling that they are acceptable to God because they are good and virtuous. Being part of such a church can make one justify oneself in this way. A church of prodigals, however, undercuts this impulse. It will not encourage its members to justify themselves because of their goodness.

The missing feature of the church in which people are friendly and good and esteemed for their good character is the overt demonstration of grace. It is the explicit sense that one is acceptable regardless of one's badness or goodness. The welcome given to newcomers is more than everyday friendliness. It is a grace-giving welcome.

A community of repenting prodigals may be closer to real faith than a community of publicly esteemed "good people."

THREE

SECRET TRAGEDIES

Most of our lives are lived in secret. What we present to other people, including those closest to us, is a veneer. Behind this veneer we live our real lives. Now and then we display something of what goes on there—a fear, perhaps, or a satisfaction. Sometimes, even, we reveal to someone we trust a feeling we are scarcely able to acknowledge to ourselves.

The prominent feature of nearly all that goes on in our secret lives is the effort to make right what feels wrong. We feel hollow and want to feel full. We feel guilty and want to feel forgiven. We remember a parental criticism and want to put salve on it. What we desire most is to resolve our tragedies.

Sometimes, maybe most of the time, we try to avoid thinking about our secret lives and the tragedies that reside there. We pretend that what we let others see is all there is. Doing this, though, is even more of a tragedy than the tragedies themselves.

What we need to do, accordingly, is to become aware of our secrets. We cannot make right our tragedies if they remain buried.

KNOWING OURSELVES

There are a number of ways in which self-knowledge is needed in the spiritual life. One of the first involves our struggle with self-centeredness. When we become aware of the specific ways in which self-centeredness displays itself, we can work on supplanting it. Only when we know the grip that self has on us can we free ourselves from it.

Some of us may find it difficult to allow ourselves to be loved by God. We may have been criticized or ridiculed when we were young, so that we feel unworthy of being loved by anyone. Knowing the source of this feeling can open the way to letting ourselves be loved by God.

Many of us are beset with a sense of guilt. At the same time, we use various strategies to evade acknowledging it—rationalization, regarding others as responsible instead of ourselves, and deliberate ignorance. Knowing these strategies requires as much subtlety as they themselves involve.

Often we possess unwanted traits, such as envy, greed, or spiritual laziness, that we may not be aware of. We may, in fact, actually not want to be aware of them and may be trying to hide them from God. When we discover this resistance in us, we are in a position to melt it and to work on ridding ourselves of the traits.

Self-knowledge can be intimidating, and because of this we strenuously avoid it. We are acutely afraid to uncover buried truths about ourselves. Yet when we feel deeply that God accepts us, we can accept ourselves and actively look for these truths.

Next to love, the main business of our lives is to know ourselves.

BROKENNESS

When we are broken, we feel helpless, both spiritually and emotionally. We are torn apart, unable to put things back together; our lives are shattered and we have lost control of the pieces. We are unable to cope and do not know how to deal with what has caused us distress.

One way in which we become broken occurs when we find ourselves failing to live up to our ideals. Another way occurs when we are tempted, give in, and later feel incapacitating remorse. A further way occurs when feelings of being unloved and worthless overwhelm us. A still further way occurs when we struggle to feel forgiven and do not quite make it.

Although we may be vaguely aware of these conditions, we do not like to think of ourselves as broken and helpless. We like to think of ourselves as being in control of our emotions. We also do not want others to think of us as broken and helpless, especially those whom we admire, for we do not want them to think we are failures. However, it is only when we admit our brokenness to ourselves that we can take in God's accepting love. This is both a spiritual and a psychological truth. In addition, admitting our brokenness to others whom we trust may help us to accept God's love.

These thoughts about brokenness imply that in a church, broken people should feel safe in admitting their brokenness to others, who in turn respond with healing touches of grace.

Only those who are aware that their lives have fallen apart can be remade.

SECRET TRAGEDIES

Psychologist Paul Tournier wrote, "There is a secret tragedy in every heart." The kind of tragedy he was referring to is not a one-time catastrophe, such as a car accident or a job loss, but a long-term tragedy that we are afraid to admit either to others or to ourselves.

This kind of tragedy may spring from discontent with our bodies. Perhaps we are too tall or too short, too thin or too big, and a little ugly; maybe our teeth stick out or we are afflicted with a handicap or a hereditary disease. Some of us are victims of people whom we have trusted; we may have been criticized or abused, physically or sexually, and the painful memories haunt us. Some of us undergo psychological trauma; perhaps we have a loneliness that comes and goes but never seems to leave. We may be in constant despair, or in continual anxiety about whether we are good enough. This anxiety may eat away at our outlook on life. False guilt may plague us or we may wrestle with sharp jabs of conscience for real guilt. Other kinds of inner pain may torment us.

All of us go through life not telling some things to anyone, and we all go through life not telling some things even to ourselves. I want to suggest five ways of dealing with these secret tragedies.

One way to make our tragedies bearable is to realize that others accept us as we are. When we know that someone loves us—even if that person does not know about our inner trauma—we are able to get through life in spite of it.

Another remedy occurs when someone else to whom we have confided our pain identifies with it. The model here is the counseling relationship. In a good counseling relationship, the greater part of the healing takes place because the counselor feels the pain of the counseled. When the counseled becomes aware that the counselor is feeling her pain, she becomes better able to live with it.

Perhaps something like this goes on when we realize that God identifies with us. The Old Testament prophet, Isaiah, declared, "We are healed by the punishment he suffered, made whole by the blows he received" (Is 53:5). God takes our tragedies upon himself, this affirmation seems to imply. The healing we feel because we know he identifies with us may be the psychological counterpart to the theological truth in the atonement.

A third remedy, if we have been betrayed, is to forgive the one who has betrayed us. If we do not do so, bitterness and resentment may fester inside us and erupt now and then. We may even have to "forgive" God in a certain sort of way, if we find ourselves angry at him.

A fourth remedy is to accept ourselves, and if need be, to forgive ourselves. We will not be able to live with ourselves if we do not accept ourselves in the same way God does—without reserve and without ulterior demands.

A final remedy is to give ourselves away, to bring healing to others, to touch them, to care about them self-forgetfully. Doing this heals us.

I do not want to give the impression that these remedies are easy. Our secret tragedies may be the most difficult situations we have to deal with. We may find ourselves in a life and death struggle with them, and we may wrestle with them throughout our lives. However, though the remedies come hard, they are worth it.

To unveil our tragedies requires both courage and grace—the former in ourselves and the latter in recipients of our unveiling.

BETRAYAL BY PARENTS

I have been listening to students over the years, and one of the things they have been telling me is that their parents have betrayed them in a number of ways. Some of them have been criticized, not just occasionally, but repeatedly and strongly. Some have been hit and pushed, or locked into a closet. Some have been sexually abused. Some have been neglected by the persons whom they most expected to care about them. A few have been abandoned and don't know where their parents are. A couple have had a father who killed himself. Some of their parents have died naturally, and although that is not betrayal, it feels like it.

They also have been telling me what their feelings are. They have painful memories about what has gone on, memories which haunt them and bubble up and hurt so much that they feel like screaming, and sometimes they do. They feel guilty for what has happened; they feel that it is their fault that they were criticized, hit, raped, or abandoned. They also feel rejected, unloved, and very insecure. Sometimes they are angry about what happened—angry at their parents, at God, and at life in general. They have wanted the offending parent to die, and on occasion have almost killed him. They get depressed, sometimes so much so that they want to kill themselves, and they have nearly succeeded at times.

These feelings are intense and often wreak havoc. Those who have them are reluctant to tell others about these feelings, and yet they cannot keep them bottled up.

What can we do if we are victims? One thing we can do is realize that we are not guilty for what happened. It is not our fault that our mother criticized us, that our father abused us, that our parents divorced each other, that they hit us, abandoned us, or drank too much.

Another thing we can do is realize that we are not alone. There are others like us who have been victims of a similar betrayal, some of whom are likely to be our present friends. Another is to find someone who cares about us and absorb that person's caring. Still another is to find someone to talk to about what happened—a trusted friend or a counselor.

I do not want to recommend that we forgive the person who wronged us, at least not now, for we may have to work through denial and anger first. Forgiveness can be a long term goal. Dealing with what happened may take years, even decades.

What can non-victims do to help victims? We can listen nonjudgmentally and be a friend. Sometimes simply being a friend, showing that we care about another, helps a person deal with wounds that we know nothing about. We can realize that it takes time and hard work for a victim to come to grips with what happened. We can make ourselves become the kind of person who wants to know about another person's hurts and pains and who feels them when we are told about them. By doing so, we will be bearing their burdens.

Forgiving a parent for betrayal means recognizing that we cannot change what happened—and being willing to move beyond it.

THE HEALING POWER OF LOVE

Many of us have been wounded. Perhaps we have bad memories from childhood. We may have been rejected by someone, criticized, abused, unloved by our parents, laughed at, or ridiculed. Perhaps we are guilty for something we have done and for which we are now ashamed. Perhaps we have negative attitudes about ourselves, with strong feelings of failure or worthlessness because we do not seem to fit in or measure up to the standards of our parents, friends, or church. Perhaps we are plagued by fears of the dark, of coming home to an empty house, or of not doing well at work. Perhaps we are pulled in opposite directions spiritually, feeling like failures here, too. All of these hurt, sometimes sharply, but more often like a dull, nagging headache.

Being loved heals these wounds. The memories, though not disappearing, lose their sting. The gnawing jabs of guilt cease. The negative feelings dissipate, the fears lose their power, and the sense of failure melts.

Oddly enough, loving others also heals our wounds. There is something about giving ourselves away that salves our hurts.

What does it feel like to be healed? We feel less pain. We do not feel so debilitated and incapacitated. The worn out feeling that comes from dealing with bad memories, guilt, and a sense of worthlessness disappears. We feel like laughing. We no longer feel alienated. We feel free and "released."

The wonderful truth about communities of faith is that they can be purveyors of healing. Though it may not be overtly evident, those in such communities have been wounded. If we think of our contacts with them as opportunities to heal, they will change through our love. And so will we.

> ### The severest wounds require the most love.

THE ULTIMATE LONELINESS AND ITS REMEDY

Loneliness is one of the most unpleasant conditions we can experience. We crave to be with people, receive attention from them, know that others care about us, and have friends. When we don't get these—or think that we don't—loneliness results.

We do a variety of things to stave off loneliness. We talk with people, do things with friends, go on dates, participate in group activities, make friends, and get married. These methods work fairly well for most people.

There is a different kind of loneliness for which the usual remedies will not work. This is an aloneness that cannot be overcome simply by being with others or by making friends. It is an ultimate loneliness from which none of us can escape, even though all of us try. It is the loneliness of guilt, the loneliness of death, and the loneliness of trying to find meaning for our lives.

Consider the loneliness of guilt. We sometimes try to assuage guilt in the same way we relieve our everyday loneliness, but although being with others may take away our everyday loneliness, it will not take away our guilt. We must deal with our guilt alone.

There are other ways we try to avoid facing the awful reality of guilt. We deny it, avoid thinking about it, imagine ourselves being pretty nice people who deserve respect and admiration, strive for success, minimize guilt's gravity, and rationalize it away. None of these work.

The same is true of death. Here, too, we try to escape our aloneness by surrounding ourselves with people. Ivan Ilyich, in Leo Tolstoy's *The Death of Ivan Ilyich*, did just that, but it didn't help. Tolstoy writes that as Ivan Ilyich lay dying, he had an "isolation in the midst of a populous city among numerous friends and relatives, an isolation that could not have been greater anywhere, either in the depths of the sea or the bowels of the earth."[4] What Ivan Ilyich discovered is that we can surround ourselves on our death beds with family and friends, but that it is still we who do the dying.

There are numerous other ways we try to avoid the loneliness of death. We say to ourselves, sometimes quite consciously, that it is other people who die, not ourselves. Or we say, "I shall live to be eighty-five," "I will never get into a fatal accident," or "I will never have to fight in a war." We entertain great hopes for our lives, blissfully unaware that death, no matter when it occurs, will some-day interrupt our cherished plans. Again, the terrible truth is that death comes to us all, and each one of us must undergo it quite alone.

The same is true for finding meaning for our lives. We cannot surround ourselves with friends and expect that the meaning we perceive in them will somehow transfer itself to us. Amazingly, we do just this. Of course, we never think this consciously, for if we did we would immediately see through it. Yet we hang onto the half-conscious thought that being with people, doing things with them, and talking with them will give meaning to our lives. This may mitigate our everyday loneliness, but it will not by itself confer meaning on our lives.

There are other ways we avoid the loneliness of finding meaning. We assume that certain ideals are legitimate, without explicitly adopting them as our own. We let social expectations mold our lifestyles without choosing a lifestyle ourselves. We resolutely cling to the hope that our lives have meaning even if we become vaguely aware that they do not, because choosing meaning is often more frightening than drifting along in our comfortable niches. Yet, again, the truth is that giving our lives an overall direction must be done alone.

It is a frightening thing to feel the loneliness of guilt, death, and trying to find life's meaning. We feel that there is nothing we can do to escape these on our own. A certain anguish, mixed with a sense of helplessness, overtakes us. If this loneliness were the final truth about human existence, our anguish would turn into despair—incapacitating despair about the meaning and value of our whole lives.

If the loneliness of guilt were ultimate, if, that is, there were no way to remedy our guilt except by our own resources, we would be condemned to live with an intolerable and non removable burden. If the loneliness of death were ultimate, if there were no way we could come to terms with our deaths except by our own ineffectual devices, we would be unable to escape the terror that the very thought of death can provoke in us. If there were no way to find meaning except by our own unguided ingenuity, we would be doomed to agonizing uncertainty and doubt about the value of our lives.

But loneliness is not ultimate. It is not the final truth about human existence. There is something that is even more ultimate and final, and that is that God is with us. Communion is more ultimate than isolation. The Incarnation is a symbol of this. No, it is more than a symbol—it is the real thing. The Incarnation is the togetherness that remedies the loneliness of guilt, death, and finding meaning.

Our guilt is no longer an intolerable and a non-removable burden, for we are offered pardon and renewal. Our deaths no longer are an unbearable terror, for we do not die alone. Finding meaning is no longer fraught with uncertainty and doubt, for the One who fashioned us and comes to us gives us genuine meaning.

Because loneliness is not the ultimate truth about our condition, we can have joy instead of despair, and because God is the remedy for our loneliness, we do not have to deny our guilt, we do not have to run from death, we do not have to avoid the question of meaning. We can face these head on, knowing that there is someone else with us who will make things come out right. This is, indeed, good news.

Everyday good news occasions temporary delight, but cosmic good news engenders long-lasting joy.

FOUR

Comfort That Money Cannot Buy

Our ground-level desires are so intense that we will do almost anything to satisfy them. We even try to satisfy them by buying things. It is not that we say to someone, "I think I will go out tonight and get some ultimate security" or "Let's go buy immortality for ourselves." If we actually said these we no doubt would recognize the absurdity of what we were about to do. No, our agenda is hidden. We prefer it that way, for otherwise we would be pained by knowing our condition.

The truth is that we are lost and need to be found, dying and need to be saved. "Lost" and "saved" have not been used much in recent decades in some circles, perhaps because of their associations, but they are perfectly good words. They pinpoint exactly what needs to be said about our attempts to buy what cannot be bought.

"WHY DO YOU WANT TO DIE?"

The Old Testament prophet, Ezekiel, depicts God as saying to the Israelites, "Give up all the evil you have been doing, and get yourselves new minds and hearts. Why do you Israelites want to die?" (Ez 18:31).

We have two reactions to the thought of getting a new heart. The first is that something in us wants one. We want more love in our lives, desiring to receive it and to give it. We want to be aware of the divine more. We desire to be sensitive to spiritual matters, to touch others' lives, and to give up destructive habits. We want love, freedom from inner turbulence, and a less constricted life. We seek forgiveness, are attracted to the self-forgetful praise of God that the Psalmist sometimes talks about, and crave to experience the mystery of God's greatness.

Our second reaction is that we resist having a new heart. We push newness away and shut down, as if we want a living death. Even though we want more love, we also resist receiving it and giving it. Even though we want to be aware of the divine more, we want less awareness as well. Though we desire to be sensitive to spiritual matters, to touch others' lives, and to give up destructive habits, we also want to remain numb and just go through the motions of being spiritual. We want to be self-contained and isolated, so we push others away and cling to destructive habits. Though we desire love, inner peace and a fuller life, we also want to continue with our self-justification. We like worrying and prefer a narrow life to a full one. Though we seek forgiveness, we also flee it; though we are attracted to self-forgetful praise, we also want to stay within ourselves; and though we desire to be awestruck by God, we also close ourselves to doing so.

"Why do you want to die?" is a haunting question. In Ezekiel it is a judgment question, as if God is pointing at us and speaking with condemnation. It is also a loving question, however, as if God has his arm around our shoulders and is speaking with tenderness.

Closing ourselves down spiritually is like killing ourselves—in both we cut ourselves off from all that is alive and good and beautiful.

SPIRITUAL DANGER

The likelihood of being a victim is four to a hundred times greater if one lives in a large city, and the likelihood is even higher if one lives in the danger zone of a city. For 1991, the number of reported violent crimes in many Illinois suburbs was lower than one hundred per 100,000 residents, and in some suburban towns it was lower than twenty-five. In contrast, for Chicago the number of violent crimes was over 2500 per 100,000 residents.

Most people do not need statistics to know about this contrast. They would feel safer in suburbs. They could go for walks after dark without fear and would not put iron bars over their windows. If they were to take a stroll through infamous sections of inner cities, they would feel the danger.

Yet there are different kinds of danger in suburbs of many large cities—nonphysical dangers that, unlike violence, are not open and apparent. People living in suburbs are often more financially secure than those living in inner cities. The resulting danger is that those who live in suburbs will be infected with "affluentism"—the feeling of disdain toward those with fewer possessions. Those who have this feeling are likely to think that they are privileged because of their wealth and are more inclined to believe that they deserve respect for having it.

Suburbs are often segregated, and consequently another danger is that some will feel that being white is normal and that being nonwhite is abnormal. People with this feeling are more likely to forget that there are groups of people living not too far away who have felt themselves to be on the receiving end of racial discrimination. They will have a tendency not to know about unemployment, poverty, and educational disadvantage. They may also begin to have a suspicious or unwelcoming attitude toward nonwhites who want to live in their suburbs.

"Jobism" and "statusism" are also dangers present in suburbs. These are the feelings that holding certain kinds of jobs makes one possess worth and that having a certain social position makes one better than those lower on the social scale.

These dangers are, to be sure, present no matter where we live. However, they are especially present in wealthy, white, and socially elite settings, whether these be in suburbs, small towns, or pockets of large cities. The mere association with the wealthy, the white, and the socially elite tends to shape our values, often without our being aware of it. Even for those who are attuned to spirituality this is so.

Moreover, affluentism, racism, jobism, and statusism can affect the way we think God regards us. They can make us think that God regards us highly because of our wealth, race, job, or social position. We would, of course, disavow any such dependence. And we would disavow being influences adversely by the setting in which we live. But the insidious nature of these dangers is that they seep into us in spite of such disavowals.

The remedy for physical danger is constant vigilance. It is the same for spiritual danger. We must be alert to conditions that subtly undermine our faith.

> **If we want to know to what our hearts are attuned, we can look at the dangers we most fear.**

CONSUMPTION

The message that television and magazine advertisements convey to us is that if we do not buy, we will not be fulfilled. Others will admire us if we buy. We will be attractive to persons of the opposite sex. The best life is one filled with a great deal of quality possessions. If we buy, we will obtain worth and esteem.

Why does this message continue to be disseminated? Perhaps the answer is that buying and possessing fulfill a basic need in us. They brings us esteem and a sense of worth, and fill our emptiness.

One of the starkest declarations in Jesus' Sermon on the Mount is, "You cannot serve God and wealth" (Mt 6:24).

The point here is both theological and psychological. If we are consumed by the message of the advertisements, we cannot also set our affection on "things above." If we set our affection on spiritual matters, we will not be gripped by the need to consume.

What does it mean to direct our affection to things above, to seek first God's values? It means that these will be the focus of our attention, our dominant interest, our loyalty, what we want most, our passion. We will be hungry and thirsty for them; they will be part of our basic drives.

When we direct our affection to things above, we will no longer need to buy in order to fill the emptiness within. We are already full. It is not so much a matter of resisting the impulse to buy, but of the impulse being squeezed out because we are filled with the eternal.

It may be that some of us will want to stop watching commercial television so that our sense of eternity is not insidiously undermined by the ads that are designed to make us pack our closets and kitchens with possessions.

> The trouble with making consumption a dominant motif of our lives is that what we consume does not fill our inexhaustible emptiness.

POSSESSIONS

One of the things for which we use our possessions is to obtain psychological and spiritual sustenance. We want security, and having a certain number of possessions gives us this. We want to feel that we are strong and impregnable, that nothing can afflict us or undermine our well-being. Obtaining possessions is a large part of feeling in control of our lives.

We also want status. We want to boast, at least to ourselves, and owning things of the right sort allows us to do this. Our drive to justify ourselves works itself out through what we own.

In addition, our possessions give us an identity. They are part of our self-concept and define who we conceive ourselves to be. They are, indeed, often the central part of our self-image.

Finally, possessions can produce greed. Although we usually think of greed as what incites us to acquire things, it works the other way as well—possessing things feeds our greed. Greed is rarely understood to be a vice in the United States, perhaps because we are so wealthy. We pounce on what we regard as clear and obvious wrongdoing, but openly display greed, forgetting that the medievals regarded it as deadly and that "life does not consist in the abundance of possessions." Those who think of sexual impurity as one of the worst sins but never mention greed do not remember that the apostle Paul put them both onto the same list: "Fornication and impurity of any kind, or greed, must not even be mentioned among you, as is proper among saints" (Eph 5:3).[5]

The sustenance we receive from possessions is sometimes true and sometimes false. Who can gainsay a measure of security, and why should we not obtain identity from what we own? What we do with material security, however, is rely on it in an absolute way. It is as if eternity hangs on the amount we own. We invest our whole identity in the kinds of things we possess, with little thought of where our eternal identity rests. And though we can own things without boasting of them or without using them to justify our existence (so we tell ourselves), we cannot easily do so. In sum, we use our possessions to run from God.

What are some antidotes? One is to accept God's love as the foundation of our lives. With love we will feel secure and our self-concept will be tied to God. As a result, we will not feel the need to use what we own to justify our existence, nor will we be impelled to base our self-image entirely on something other than God.

Another antidote is to try giving away some of our possessions. If we cannot do this without feeling insecure or without losing our sense of identity, then we know we are getting our security and identity only from them and not also from God. "It is better to go through life without a right hand knowing that we will be made whole beyond the grave than it is to be whole now but maimed then" (Mt 5:30).

Finally, we can adopt the slogan, "We cannot take them with us." Realizing that death forces us to leave all of our possessions behind is a powerful way of driving us to God's grace.

Money is like sex—both a delight and a snare.

"YOU CANNOT TAKE IT WITH YOU"

When someone says, "You cannot take it with you," they are usually referring to possessions, but could just as easily be referring to other features of our lives. We can't, for example, take our social roles with us when we die, or our skin color or the activities by which we identify ourselves or the fact that we are admired by numerous people or that we have become important in the groups to which we belong.

When we think about the fact that we cannot take any of these with us when we die, we can discover what we are attached to. If we were to have a strong aversion to not being able to take one of these with us, we could infer that we are strongly attached to it. If we were not to have a strong aversion, then we would not have an strong attachment. Most of us, for most of the features of our lives, probably fall into the first category. We feel almost a wrenching repugnance to having to leave behind the roles we have so carefully built up, the successes in which we have invested so much energy, and the admiration that keeps us fueled.

We can also discover our real identities by the same method. We can notice what is left when we imagine ourselves not being able to take our roles, successes, and sources of admiration with us. In this way, we are able to distinguish our real selves from our false selves. Our false selves are the fronts we present to others, the temperament that we wrongly convince ourselves we have—the wood, hay, and stubble that we imagine ourselves to be, but which will be burned from us at death.

Using this imaginative technique does two things: It vividly demonstrates how much we justify our existence with our possessions, social roles, admiration, and achievements, and it pushes us to find our identity in God, for there is nothing else to rely on when the possessions, social roles, and admiration have disappeared. When we find our identity in God, we give up the guises by which we conceive our identity and let faith become the core of our character.

> Some of us may not discover our true selves until after we die.

MUFFLERS

In his perceptive book *Until Justice and Peace Embrace*, Nicholas Wolterstorff remarks that "what so often happens is that in countless ingenious ways the sharp sound of the Word of God is muffled so as to protect the status quo."[6]

It is not surprising that this is so. The pressure to conform to society's values is strong, not so much because society consciously exerts this pressure, but because there is deep within us a desire to be accepted by other people, even if doing so means muffling our values and convictions. In addition, we are fallen creatures, and at times we resist the incisive voice of God. It is sometimes just too uncomfortable to hear, and it is much easier to float along with the status quo.

Wealth is one muffler we use to blunt the sharp sound of God's call. We can use wealth to take the edge off the scriptural injunction to seek first the kingdom of God by saying that it is our attitude toward possessions that matters and not the amount we have. This no doubt is true, but too often we use it as an excuse to muffle the fact that the possession of wealth is dangerous to our spiritual condition.

National power is another muffler. Part of the United States' political and cultural milieu is that we are the strongest nation in the world. We have enough nuclear weapons to kill all human, animal, and plant life on earth a dozen times, and we are proud of this power because it makes us superior to every other country. We forget that God wants humility, not power; love, not demonstration of strength. To be sure, national security is needed, but its exaltation can muffle God's clear insistence that we are to be peacemakers.

Still another muffler is the pursuit of personal happiness. God surely wants us to be happy. There are numerous people whose lives need a good deal more happiness. Yet if one makes the pursuit of happiness the prime goal of one's life, God's bidding for us to exhibit sacrificial love and to work for justice will be muffled.

Social class and skin color are also mufflers. They can stifle the truth that we are a family of equals no matter what characteristics we have.

Other mufflers include television advertisements, which can numb us to spiritual values; the mass media, which can skew our perceptions; and even expectations by fellow believers, which can distort our vision of what is important in life. It is so much easier sometimes to let these deaden the piercing urgency of God's declarations.

Some muffling gives us genuine comfort, but other muffling gives us only false comfort.

BUILDING BIGGER BARNS

In the parable of the bigger barns, a man tears down his barns and builds bigger ones so that he can store his growing quantity of grain: "The land of a rich man produced abundantly. And he thought to himself, 'What should I do, for I have no place to store my crops?' Then he said, 'I will do this: I will pull down my barns and build larger ones, and there I will store all my grain and my goods'" (Lk 12:16-18).

In a contemporary context, the parable might be recast so as to feature someone selling her house so that she can buy a bigger one, or it might involve someone buying nicer furniture, purchasing higher grade clothes, adding to her savings account, investing in mutual funds, buying a higher level car, traveling to a foreign country, or purchasing a cottage.

The first point to notice about this parable is that it speaks to something in each of us: a nearly irresistible desire to have more. This desire is evidenced in a number of ways: shopping trips being recreational activities, our need level rising as we get older, feeling empty if we haven't purchased something for awhile, wanting the nice things our friends have. Although we publicly denounce opulence, we secretly would like to own a million-dollar home with a pond and enough cash to hire caretakers for the lawn. The truth is that when our barns aren't big enough anymore, instead of getting rid of the excess, we want to put up another barn to store the overflow.

A second point to notice about the parable is that the issue in it is whether we are connected to God. What it says is that this connection is undermined by the desire for bigger barns. The man was called a fool: "So it is with those who store up treasures for themselves but are not rich toward God" (Lk 12: 21). Experience confirms the point: we cannot have a desire for bigger barns and also be connected to God. We cannot be dominated by two different drives; one of them will squeeze out the other. Thus, the issue becomes, "What do we want with our lives—to build bigger barns or to be connected to God?" A voice secretly whispers to us, "Build bigger barns." If this parable is on target, we need to resist this insistent voice, or else we, too, will end up having wasted our lives filling our closets and inflating our bank accounts.

> Most of us can live just as well, perhaps even better, with much less.

COMFORT THAT MONEY CANNOT BUY

The parable of the bigger barns suggests several thoughts about buying comfort.

We possess varying kinds and degrees of discomfort, some of which are quite specific and some of which are general. Sometimes we feel dissatisfied with our clothes or our car or with something else we have. Sometimes we have a vague longing for something more without quite knowing what we want. On occasion, a certain restlessness afflicts us, and on other occasions, the feeling that we are not good enough arises in us.

To dispel this discomfort, we buy things. We buy clothes so that we will feel good about how we look and we buy cars so that we will feel admired. We also buy things to absolve guilt feelings, to satisfy our longing for something more, to quell our restlessness, and to give ourselves a sense of being good enough.

Buying comfort does not work, however, for the discomfort returns. We buy new things and more clothes. Our lives become a perpetual cycle of discomfort and buying, of longing and more buying, of restlessness and still more buying.

Is there some way to break this cycle? Can we get comfort that money cannot buy? We can, I believe, but not easily, for the impulse to buy comfort that money cannot buy is nearly intractable, and the habit of doing so is entrenched in us. What we must do is ask ourselves as we buy, "What kind of comfort am I buying with this purchase?"

> Buying comfort that money cannot buy is like eating a large bowl of Jell-O for lunch—we can do it, but we will feel hungry soon after.

FIVE

RESTLESS HEARTS

Our restlessness is an indication that something has gone wrong. What it indicates is that we have not yet entirely responded to the One who invites us to rest.

What would it be like to possess rest? We are so restless that it is hard to imagine anything different. Perhaps the best we can do is to imagine the absence of the features that make us restless. Chasing after fruitless goals, for example, would be gone. The emptiness we constantly try to avoid would also be gone. So would our discontent with nearly everything we do. In their places we would experience an uninterrupted settledness, a sense that life is full, and contentedness with what we do. It was for these that we were made, and our lives are bleak without them.

SPIRITUAL STRUGGLE

Someone once wrote that living is unspeakably hard. Frederick Douglass, the nineteenth century abolitionist, said in connection with the effort to abolish slavery, "If there is no struggle, there is no progress. . . . Men may not get all they pay for in this world; but they must certainly pay for all they get."[7]

There are a number of ways in which the life of the spirit is unspeakably hard and involves exhausting struggles. The spiritual life requires exerting effort. Some days, though, we want to relax and be a spectator, to think about life instead of actually living it. What we most want on these occasions is to retreat inside ourselves and be a spiritual hermit.

Loving, too, is unspeakably hard. To love, we must overcome self-centeredness that is wildly out of control. Succumbing to the self's inordinate demands is much more to our liking than listening to the wounds of others.

Receiving forgiveness is also extraordinarily hard. To receive forgiveness, we must peer inward at feelings and emotions we would rather not know about. We have to admit wrongs. It is far easier simply to set them aside. Often, even, we resist forgiveness as more than we can handle.

In addition, dealing with emotions frequently is too much for us. We wrestle with insecurity, loneliness, and doubt. We worry and are anxious. Sometimes we intentionally hang onto our worries and anxieties because they feel comfortable to us. At the same time, we want them gone. Even if we have quelled our inner turmoil, we are still subject to conflicting emotions.

What can we do? Perhaps the first thing is to admit that we struggle: to acknowledge that we don't always give up our worries, that we hardly ever feel like loving, that we sometimes resist forgiveness. It is enormously tempting not to admit these and to put on a fake front, pretending that everything is okay. We are so programmed to think of ourselves as living wonderful and victorious lives, defeating sin and overcoming temptation, that to admit difficulty is tantamount to admitting complete failure. We cannot deal with struggle, though, until we stop hiding it from ourselves.

We can also come to realize that life in the spirit is, indeed, hard work and that some things become harder *because* we want to live in the spirit. We just have to do the hard work that is required to get through our struggles. Nothing worthwhile is easy. There is something about chopping wood that makes us grow. "All things excellent are as difficult as they are rare," declared Spinoza, a seventeenth-century philosopher.[8]

One concrete action we can take is to surround ourselves with intimate friends who will support us even if they know nothing of our struggles. We can also overcome our fear of confessing our secrets to others; when we do, we will find that others reciprocate. Last, we can convince ourselves that the struggle is worth it.

Achieving anything of value requires 5% vision and 95% hard work.

HEAVY LOADS

There are different kinds of loads we carry, some of which we put onto ourselves and some of which are put onto us without our permission.

Dissatisfaction with our bodies is one kind of heavy load. Some of us may not be very pretty or handsome; we may have too many scars from pimples, or a shape that others disdain.

Almost all of us have a strong drive to be admired. When we feel that we are not, we have a different kind of load to carry.

Another burden consists of being victims of parental betrayal—some of us have been criticized, hit, neglected, or abused. We have painful memories, flashbacks, tons of false guilt, and a great deal of self-rejection. We may need others to help us carry these burdens.

Another kind of heavy load is the feeling that we are never good enough for anyone. We always have to be better, continually doing certain things to convince ourselves that we are okay. This feeling can become especially heavy to carry, for we do not seem able to dispel it for long. We need fresh ways of gaining esteem and new episodes of self-justification. Perhaps this load is one of the heaviest we ever carry.

Jesus knew about the heavy loads we carry, for he invited us to let him carry them: "Come to me, all you that are weary and are carrying heavy burdens, and I will give you rest" (Mt 11:28). When we accept this offer, life feels easier, we breathe a sigh of relief, skip lightheartedly, cease being bothered by our pimples, feel loved, and know that we are cared about in spite of our perceived or real deficiencies.

Some loads were meant to be carried, some not.

EMPTINESS

On an exam a student once wrote, "Every time I devote myself to any activity, it turns out to be empty. The void inside truly can only be filled by God."

This emptiness is the feeling of a lack, a void, a hollowness. It is the feeling that what we do has no significance. It differs from loneliness, though it may be accompanied by loneliness.

The first point to notice about this emptiness is that we do, indeed, feel it on occasion. Sometimes it surfaces to consciousness, but often it hovers just below full awareness.

A second point to notice is that we cannot bear to have the feeling for long. We fear having it, dread it even. We dare not let it into full consciousness, because we are afraid of the thought that our lives may be hollow at the core.

A third point to note is that we engage in various activities, both good and not so good, to try to do away with the emptiness. In fact, we use just about everything we do to make sure we do not have this painful feeling. We buy clothes, strive for recognition, obtain possessions, attend meetings, think about things—anything to get our minds off our inner condition. We listen to music, watch television, pursue projects, talk with people, engage in sex, do things to be well-liked, go to baseball or basketball games, say witty things, read, go to movies—all so that we will not feel empty.

Augustine wrote, "You have made us for yourself, and our hearts are restless until they rest in you."[9] When we find rest, we do not need to listen to the radio, buy things, or work in our yards to escape the sense of hollowness. When our hearts rest in God, we know that what we do and who we are matters.

Filling the God-shaped space within with trivial pursuits is like pouring water into a leaky bucket—they fill for a while, but eventually leave us empty.

DESPAIR

Despair comes at some point in nearly everyone's life. Sometimes it is mild and sometimes it is severe. Some people deal with it easily, but others struggle with it. The author of the Psalms probably was one of the latter. He wrote, "Out of the depths I cry to you, O Lord." "My spirit is faint," he admitted. "No one cares for me," he complained.[10]

We can fall into despair when we come to feel that there is nothing worth living for. We can fall into despair when we lose all hope and have nothing to look forward to. We can fall into despair when we feel that no one cares about us or accepts us. We can fall into despair when we come to feel our guilt and can find no way to escape from it. We can fall into despair when failure (perceived or real), criticism, or abuse causes self-rejection.

Faith is applicable to all of these. Faith gives meaning to our lives and gives us hope. It assures us that we are loved. It is able to take in forgiveness. Because of this love and forgiveness, we can accept ourselves.

I do not want to suggest that faith is an easy solution to despair. Dealing with our despair is almost always a severe struggle, sometimes of a life-and-death sort. In such cases, nothing matters to us, not even God.

What can we do when despair hits us? There are several steps we can take that may make a difference. One is to surround ourselves with people who care about us, and absorb their caring. Another is to talk to someone. Doing this may be extremely hard, for although we desperately want to talk about our despair, we find it nearly impossible to do so. Finding courage to reveal our inner lives, however, is often the beginning of a solution. A third thing to do is to diagnose the source. Those in despair often do not know what has brought on their feelings. Although knowing the source of the feelings does not automatically dispel them, it does get the "enemy" into the open so that we can aim at it better.

What can we do when despair hits other people? We can be with them and listen to them. Doing this means that we accept them without being critical. One thing we should never say or imply is, "If you had more faith, you would not be like this." Saying this just piles on more guilt and self-rejection, and those who are in despair may want faith but are unable at the time to have it.

My perception of people in communities of faith is that many undergo some kind of despair at some time or other. Often, though, our caring helps, even though we do not know others are suffering.

> Despair kills some people, but strengthens others.

ANXIETY

Iris Murdoch wrote, "We are anxiety-ridden animals."[11] This quote prompts several questions. What is the extent of our anxiety? Do we want to be free of it? What is the remedy for anxiety?

Numerous worries afflict each of us: Do other people like me? Does someone of the opposite sex notice me? How will I get all my work done? Will I have enough money? What will I do if I lose my job? Am I dressed right?

We possess deeper anxieties as well: self-worth anxiety (am I good enough?), guilt anxiety (what can I do about guilt?), suicidal anxiety (why should I keep on living when I am in so much pain?), crisis of faith anxiety (what if all I have believed about God is false?), anxiety of loneliness (what if I go to a meeting and no one notices that I am there?), moral anxiety (am I good?), meaning of life anxiety (am I wasting my life?), and death anxiety (what if I die?).

We do, indeed, want to rid ourselves of these anxieties. They drive us to seek solace in artificial palliatives which we know are not good for us. They produce more anxiety, and on the whole can ruin our lives. We want contented peace; we crave freedom from worry; we desire the kind of security that forestalls the need for us to have cares.

Yet we also cling to our worries in almost an addictive way. So entrenched are we in anxiety that far from wanting to be rid of it we feel uncomfortable when we are not worrying about something. Only some of the time do we genuinely want to be free, and rarely do we "envy the careless and innocent happiness of the birds of the air."

The first thing we can do about anxiety is to become aware of it, to notice when it controls us, and to perceive those occasions when we find comfort in worrying. If we are unaware of having an anxious look on our face, it is likely to stay there. Another thing we can do is to ask ourselves, "Why do I need to worry about this?" Asking this question impels us to see that we do not need our worries and pushes us to let go of them. Lastly, we can give our anxieties to God, letting him worry about them, knowing that he will take care of them a good deal better than we can.

Some anxiety is trivial, but some is momentous and concerns life's important realities.

DREAD

One of the feelings we can have toward God is dread. We experience dread when we think of God's perfection. We also experience dread when we realize that God has complete power over us. Together these thoughts make us afraid of God.

Dread is a blending of fear and aversion. It is an extreme uneasiness in the face of a disagreeable prospect. If we let it, the dread we feel toward God can become intense and overpowering, unable to be endured for more than a few seconds. We immediately shrink from God, avoiding him altogether or denying the cause of the dread—our moral imperfection and our helplessness. We feel it is a fearful thing to fall into the hands of the living God.

This feeling of dread comes to us on occasion even if we are people of faith. It slips into our consciousness unbidden.

The opposite of dread is a mixture of feelings—including peace and joy—but most of all, security. It is the feeling of being accepted by God, of being forgiven, of inner tranquility, of being loved unconditionally. It is the feeling we got when we sat beside our mothers when we were little, or when our fathers put us to bed, read us a story, and said a prayer. It is the feeling of assurance that everything is okay and that we will not be harmed. With this feeling, there is no trace of fear or aversion. God is no longer a threat to us.

Dread is an intensely terrifying feeling to have. It can be driven away only by an equally fervent sense of security and love.

We can scarcely think of a powerful and perfectly holy being, or of nature at its rawest, without at least a twinge of dread and terror.

SPIRITUAL TRAGEDY AND SPIRITUAL BEAUTY

Perhaps the most basic truth about human nature is its dividedness: human existence is both tragic and beautiful. Philosopher Blaise Pascal mirrors these sentiments in his memorable statement, "We are the glory and refuse of the universe."[12]

It is part of the tragedy of our existence that we resist goodness and that we hide from the One who could give us what we know we need. It is tragic that inner turmoil afflicts us and that guilt gnaws at our conscience. We are restless, sometimes desperate, occasionally feeling so much hopelessness that we can scarcely continue living. We feel pulled in opposite directions and sometimes catch ourselves with a murderous impulse. Much of what we do is done to justify ourselves, to make others think we are good. We cannot accept love, are afraid to take risks, and shrink from living the larger life we are offered.

These tragedies should evoke sorrow in us—a deep sense of regret and disappointment, perhaps even bitter lament. We are truly things to cry about, literally, when we reflect in a quiet place.

We are also things of great beauty, for in becoming new persons we are shaped into something exquisite and pleasing to observe. We have moments of genuineness. We feel real compassion for victims and come to the aid of those who are in trouble. Our words help heal another's wounds. We make efforts to love and allow ourselves to be loved. We overcome desperation. On occasion, we leave behind inordinate concern for our own welfare. We find contentment in love and not in possessions. We touch someone, set aside inner turmoil, feel whole, and take in God's larger life.

This beauty should evoke awe in us—a sense of greatness and magnificence, a splendor that we can scarcely take in, a breathtaking grandeur. We are like shining diamonds.

It is fitting to think of ourselves in this way. To do so is to possess exhilarating delight in the beauty of human existence, along with keen contentment.

These attitudes are ones that God has as well. He sees us both as living tragedies and as beautiful beings. If God could cry or smile, we would see him looking at us with a tear rolling down one of his cheeks, with a look of sorrow and anticipatory longing behind the tear, but also, as difficult as this may be to imagine, with a look of excited delight and surpassing contentment.

> We do not truly know someone until we agonize over their tragedies and cherish their magnificence. One of life's great aims is to feel more keenly both its tragedy and its beauty.

LOVING AND THE MEANING OF LIFE

One of my students once wrote,

> There have been times when I have felt very lonely and have wondered what the meaning of life is. But as I reached out of myself to others and loved

them in the way I needed to be loved, I found the meaning of life. When we are truly trying to love others and when we are thinking of them rather than ourselves, then we are far from questioning the meaning of life.

A foundational desire is to answer the question, "What is the point of my existence? What makes my life worthwhile?" It is one of the most unsettling questions we can ask, for when we do, we often get the uneasy feeling that our lives may not have meaning. We might be wasting them. We cannot live with this feeling, which makes us want to suppress the question, plunge into more living, and follow the course that we think is set for us. But the question will not go away, and in certain lonely moments it pops up again.

One answer, perhaps the only answer, is to give ourselves away. It is to lose ourselves in the lives of others, to love them in ways we need to be loved. When we do this, we find ourselves satisfied in a deep way, unlike the superficial satisfaction we get when we buy something to fill an empty feeling, do something only because it is admired by others, immerse ourselves in a lively party, or interact with a person of the opposite sex. Though these assuage our emptiness, it returns more acutely afterwards. When we love, though, the nagging question about meaning goes away.

The two great commandments—that we love God and our neighbors as ourselves—become not just duties, but internalized drives that both consume and fulfill.

The point here is not that we should love in order to be satisfied, for if we do this, we are simply using people as equipment to get something for ourselves. Moreover, the satisfaction will not come if we aim for it, even if we aim for it by loving. It is as much a psychological truth as a spiritual truth that if we try to save our lives we will really lose them, but that the result of losing our lives is finding them.

> Some things we have to aim at in order to get, while other things come to us when we aim at something else.

RESTLESS HEARTS

Carl Jung wrote, "A secret unrest gnaws at the roots of our being."[13] What is this unrest? It is both a dissatisfaction with our current state and a longing for something more. It is an emptiness and a homesickness. It is a certain wistfulness that displays itself in a faraway look on our faces when we sit quietly contemplating life.

We are restless not only when we think of the vanity of our trivial pursuits or of the largeness of eternity, but also when we engage in good activities. We wonder whether even these are all there is to life.

Often we scarcely notice our restlessness. We cover it with busyness and immerse ourselves in the needs of the day, so that the sharp, unsettling feeling will not come to consciousness, or we reach a pinnacle in an accomplishment and think we are fully satisfied. When later we vaguely glimpse its hollowness, we promptly conceive of a new pinnacle to achieve, shoving aside the feeling that is both a clue to our condition and a call from eternity. What is the remedy for restlessness? Perhaps delight in God's ways of the sort expressed in various places by the Psalmists is part of the remedy. Perhaps self-forgetful praise of God is as well—the disinterested losing of ourselves in God. And perhaps, too, the contented realization that we are loved by God plays a role in dispelling restlessness.

Can our restlessness be entirely eliminated in this life? Our inner turbulence and chasing after the wind seem to say, "No." Yet we are offered a peace that passes understanding. Perhaps, then, the life of faith is the beginning of that "something more" that we grow into, bit by bit.

Behind a driven life is a restless heart.

"COME TO ME"

In his *Practice in Christianity*, Søren Kierkegaard has a marvelous passage on Jesus' invitation to those of us who have too much to bear: "Come here to me, all you who labor and are burdened, and I will give you rest" (Mt 11:28).

> The invitation goes out, and wherever there is a crossroad, it stands still and calls. . . .
>
> It stands at the crossroad, there where temporal and earthly suffering placed its cross, and calls. Come here, all you poor and wretched, you who must slave in poverty to secure for yourselves—not a carefree but a hard future. . . . You despised and disregarded ones, whose existence no one, no one cares about, not even as much as for a domestic animal, which has more value!—You sick, lame, deaf, blind, crippled, come here!—You who are confined to your beds—yes, you come too, for the invitation has the nerve to invite the bedridden—to come!—You lepers! The invitation blasts away all distinctions in order to gather everybody together; it wants to make up for what happens as a result of distinction: the assigning to one person a place as a ruler over millions, in possession of all the goods of fortune, and to someone else a place out in the desert. . . .
>
> You sick at heart, you who only through pain learn to know that a human being has a heart in a different sense than an animal does and what it means to suffer there, what it means that a physician may be correct in saying that someone has a sound heart and yet is heartsick; you whom faithlessness deceived . . . ; all you who have been treated unfairly, wronged, insulted, and mistreated; all you noble ones who, as everyone is sure to

tell you, well-deservedly reaped the reward of ingratitude . . . ; all you sacrifices to cunning and deceit and slander and envy, whom villainy singled out and cowardice deserted . . . —come here! The invitation stands at the crossroad, where death distinguishes death from life. Come here, all you sorrowing ones, you who, burdened, labor in futility! . . .

The invitation stands at the crossroad, there where the road of sin veers away from the hedge row of innocence—come here, you are so close to him; one single step onto the other way and you are so infinitely far away from him. . . . The invitation stands at the crossroad, there where the way of sin turns more deeply into sin. Come here, all you who are lost and gone astray, whatever your error and sin. . . . Oh, turn around, turn around, come here; do not shrink from the difficulty of retreat, no matter how hard it is. . . .

Come here, all, all, all of you; with him is rest. And he makes no difficulty; he does only one thing: he opens his arms.[14]

As Kierkegaard so eloquently declares, the invitation to find rest is meant for all of us. When I think of this fact, however, I tend not to think that it is meant for me. It is, though, for I too have labored and need quiet restoration. I too have a wounded heart that needs to be loved. I too have anxiously fled from God and need reconciliatory peace. The invitation is not just for other people, those who are sick, guilty, and bowed down. It is for each of us who is heavily laden—all of us.

> **It is sometimes harder to accept a simple invitation to unburden ourselves than it is to carry the burden.**

SIX

LETTING OTHERS LOVE US

There is good reason to think that the hardest thing about pursuing the life of faith is being selfless. We are driven by our egos and can scarcely control them; we have numerous needs of our own to satisfy and little energy for others' needs; we like getting attention and praise and do not much like giving them.

The meditations in this section point out that there is equally good reason to think that allowing ourselves to be loved is at least as hard as being selfless. Since one of the central truths about God is that he loves us, the importance of this fact is immediately established. We need, accordingly, to reflect on what it is to allow ourselves to be loved and on what the obstacles to doing so are. We also need to focus more of our energy on actually being loved. Doing this, far from making us more self-centered, makes us less so. Odd as it may seem, we give love more when we let ourselves be loved more.

ACCEPTING FORGIVENESS

Accepting someone's forgiveness seems easy compared to forgiving someone who has wronged us. Yet there are "requirements" of accepting forgiveness that make it harder than we may originally have supposed.

The first is that we must recognize what we have done that needs forgiving. Doing this means looking into ourselves, peering into hiding places, investigating dark secrets. It means opening ourselves to the burning yet loving gaze of God. We desperately do not want to admit to God or to ourselves what we know is inside us, for we have an irresistible impulse to feel good about ourselves. It is stretching things only a little to say that we would rather die than confess that we need forgiveness.

The second requirement is that we must recognize the cost to the forgiver. We must be aware of the pain we have caused to someone we care about, and we must also be aware of how hard it may be for that person to forgive us in spite of the pain we have caused.

The third requirement is that we must want to change. Could we genuinely accept forgiveness if we secretly wanted to repeat what we know we need forgiveness for? The difficult part here is that we often still desire to do the very thing we know needs forgiving. This desire may be as strong as the attraction of food to a starving person.

The fourth requirement is that we must resist the impulse to pay back the offended person. Our impulse, when we know we have wronged someone, is to "pay back" our wrong by doing something good. This is the motive behind self-justification, a motive that is at the bottom of much that we do. We strive to show others how good we are, how successful, intelligent, and attractive. However, it is a motive that accepting forgiveness will have nothing to do with. Accepting forgiveness requires sheer gratitude and unfeigned acceptance of the offered forgiveness.

John states, "If we confess our sins, he who is faithful and just will forgive us our sins and cleanse us from all unrighteousness" (1 Jn 1:9). This is a sure truth, but the "if" is one of the most tortuous ifs of all.

The forgiveness God offers is free, yet costly.

LETTING OTHERS LOVE US

The question, "Do we let others love us?" is significant for several reasons. The first is that a basic feature of the life of faith is allowing ourselves to be loved. This follows from the fact that the life of faith must be lived in community, both with God and with others of like mind, and community requires interaction—the giving and receiving of love. Moreover, a basic human need is to be loved. If we do not or cannot let others love us, we will not be able to live. Those who are unable to feel the care that others have toward them are likely simply to shrivel up, wanting even to die. Lastly, loving requires that we ourselves have been loved. If we are unable to let others love us, it is improbable that we will be able to give love.

Letting others love us is difficult, though. When we let another person love us, we must let that person know us.

We are afraid to let anyone else know us, because we are fearful that she might discover something which would cause her to reject us. The same is true of God. Even though our minds may tell us that God accepts us in spite of the secrets we would rather he not know, our hearts still feel reserve and trepidation.

In addition, we feel that we do not deserve to be loved. We feel a need to earn what we get in life, and being loved is like being given an unearned gift. We want to do something in return, not as a way of expressing gratitude, but as a way of paying for the gift, so we do not allow ourselves to be loved as we are. Instead, we work for love by making ourselves worthy of others' admiration, by showing that we are successful, by acting in ways we think others would approve. However, it would not be love we get in return for these, but payment.

Some of us find it difficult to receive others' love because we grew up in families where there was little closeness. We feel most comfortable keeping others at a distance, because that is what feels normal to us. We do not know what it is like for God to be close to us, for we have not experienced anything like it, and when we perceive him getting closer than we are accustomed, we push him away.

Others of us feel that we cannot let anyone get close to us because those whom we trusted in the past have betrayed us or criticized us or did not give us approval when we most needed it. To avoid a repetition, we stay away from others emotionally, saying to ourselves that the other person does not really matter anyway.

Still others of us have become perfectionists. We need to be perfect in order to feel acceptable to ourselves. Letting someone love us "just because" feels strange.

Men may find it hard to receive love because they have been socialized to be strong and independent. Letting themselves be loved feels weak and wimpy.

The first thing we can do to overcome these obstacles is to become aware of them. When we see that what we do is motivated by a desire to earn God's esteem, the way is open to let God love us without condition. When we discover that our inability to let others into our lives comes from fear of rejection, we can seek out others who will not criticize us and who will have regard for us independently of our performance.

Another thing we can do is to practice receiving little things—a smile, a touch, a letter. We may, indeed, have to practice a long time on little things before we feel ready to move to larger things. What seems like the easiest thing in the world is really the hardest, but with work it can be obtained.

> Taking in love is as hard as giving it. Those who can genuinely do one can also do the other.

MATTERING TO GOD

There are times in our lives when we find ourselves disintegrating. Despair and hopelessness set in. Doubts about the reality of God, about ourselves, and about the meaning of life haunt us.

At one point in his life, Alan Jones experienced these things. In his book *Exploring Spiritual Direction: An Essay on*

Christian Friendship, he describes one of the occurrences that helped him get through his crisis.

> Part of the rescue operation was a summons from the dean of the seminary to go for an afternoon walk with him across the moors. I had no choice; walks with the dean (or principal as he was called) were part of a seminarian's lot. He was an extraordinary and powerful personality. I have since come to realize that he is an extremely complex man whose own psychological and spiritual wounds helped to make him the man he was and is. At the time I had no real notion of his own hurts. I received nothing but receptivity and love and it was this which influenced me deeply. It was as if he could see into my deepest self. He was able to show me that God loved me all the way through. He was the bearer of the miracle that I mattered. This doctrine that I matter, that people matter, was and is the hardest thing for me to believe. My struggle with other aspects of Christian belief are insignificant compared with the difficulty I have in accepting that I am loved.
>
> My walk with the principal across the moors was one of the many incidents that convinced me that I was loved, and it was this that continued the healing process of breaking up the cloud of doubt that had paralyzed me.
>
> Someone stretched out his hand to me at a time when I couldn't tolerate myself. I was touched by another in the fellowship of the Church and told (not in words) that I mattered. That is what brought me to Christianity and keeps me Christian: the miracle that I matter.[15]

This passage drives home the truth that we have an intense need to know that we are loved. Our search for meaning involves showing ourselves that we matter. If we could not know this, we would not find life worth living.

Most of us, though, perhaps even all of us, struggle with accepting God's love. We find it difficult to believe that we matter to him. Though we may have easily embraced God's love at one time, sooner or later doubts creep in.

Part of what it means to say that God loves us is to say that we matter to him. God forgives us because we matter to him, and God's grace consists in our mattering to God. He loves us all the way through.

Knowing that we matter to God brings a profound satisfaction. It calms us, soothes us, dispels inner turmoil; it diffuses despair, heals our hurts, infuses hope in us, and enables us to live with ourselves. For some of us, this knowledge has kept us alive when living itself seemed a futile endeavor.

Sometimes, we come to feel that we matter to God because people have shown us that we matter to them, and no doubt others have come to feel that they matter to God because we have shown them that they matter to us. Often we do not know what far-reaching effects we have on those whom we love. The seminary dean probably had little inkling of the revolutionary consequences his routine walk had on Alan Jones.

Our burdens weigh less when we sense that we matter to God.

THE CONSEQUENCES OF ACCEPTING LOVE

When we accept the love that another offers us, various things happen. We are drawn to the one who loves us. Our fears and anxieties dissolve, and our worries and burdens no longer overwhelm us. We feel free to be ourselves instead of being what we believe others want us to be. We begin to love people with a spontaneous overflow. We are able to live with ourselves; our self-rejection, sense of failure, and guilt are dissipated. We accept ourselves. We do not need false satisfactions any more, such as television, success, destructive sex, or possessions—the thousand distractions we use to fill the emptiness within. We feel ourselves changing, almost in spite of ourselves. The impediments to becoming a new person are chased away by love.

Perhaps the foundation—no, perhaps the very essence—of a life of faith is accepting God's love. Perhaps the focus of our energies should not be on what we can do to please God or on trying to fulfill all the commands we believe he has given us, but on allowing ourselves to be loved. There is a mystery here: allowing ourselves to be loved changes us without our trying to change.

Renewal comes more from allowing ourselves to be loved than from effort and exertion.

LOVING AND FORGIVING OURSELVES

The dilemma involved in loving and forgiving ourselves is that these are among the hardest things to do, yet they are also among the most significant things we can do. They are, in fact, almost requirements for living.

It is hard to love and forgive ourselves because we have a disposition to love conditionally instead of unconditionally, and this is as true of love directed toward ourselves as it is of love directed toward others. When we love ourselves conditionally, we feel that we have to be successful, have certain qualities, and act in conformity with our expectations for ourselves. Since we are acutely aware that we do not possess these qualities and do not live up to these expectations, we find ourselves unlovable.

As evidence of this, note that we often think of ourselves as better than others in specific ways in order to compensate for feeling inferior, which is a sign that we are not accepting ourselves as we are. Note also that we sometimes act in exemplary ways in order to compensate for not being able to forgive ourselves. Note as well that we downplay our achievements or make self-critical remarks or cannot accept praise. The truth is that each of has a morass of negative feelings about ourselves.

Yet if we do not love and forgive ourselves, we will not be able to live with ourselves. We will be restless because we will be searching for ways to make ourselves appear good to ourselves. We will be unable to give ourselves to others selflessly, for we will act in ways that we think enhance our status with ourselves. When we love ourselves unconditionally, however, we can love others without having to get something in return.

In addition, loving and forgiving ourselves is connected to our ability to accept God's forgiveness. In a perceptive observation on forgiveness, Malcolm France writes, "If guilt is to be healed, the victim must be reconciled to himself. . . . The forgiveness which others would give him is blocked by his inability to forgive himself."[16]

This statement suggests that in order to accept God's forgiveness we need to forgive ourselves. Forgiving ourselves involves the same things that accepting God's forgiveness involves. It involves admitting to ourselves that we have fallen short. Doing this is difficult because we desperately do not want to admit, even to ourselves (especially to ourselves), that we have failed. It also involves accepting ourselves in spite of our having fallen short. We become reconciled to ourselves and love ourselves no matter what. We do not have to be successful or have certain qualities or act in specific ways in order to accept ourselves.

Perhaps there is a two-way connection between forgiving ourselves and accepting God's forgiveness. We cannot forgive ourselves unless we experience God's forgiveness, and we cannot embrace God's forgiveness unless we have forgiven ourselves.

The assertion that we should love our neighbors as ourselves means at least that we should love ourselves in the same way we should love others, not more but not less either, with the same tenderness and accepting spirit we offer to wounded and broken acquaintances, for we, too, are wounded and broken.

Conditional self-love is as malignant as conditional neighbor love.

SELF-WORTH

It is legitimate for us to believe that we have worth, for it is legitimate to believe what is true, and the truth is that we do have worth. God made us and we are valuable to him. However, a salient fact about most of us is that we do not always feel that we have worth. In fact, we often have negative attitudes toward ourselves, and a large share of what we do, think, and desire consists of trying to combat these negative attitudes.

A number of sources contribute to the feeling that we do not have worth. Parental criticism can make us feel critical toward ourselves. The same is true of criticism from friends or acquaintances, even if we do not know them very well. The person who has been physically or sexually abused by her parents feels a great deal of shame. Parental neglect can also bring about the same feeling. Not obtaining high grades in school can make us feel inadequate, and seeing someone who is better than we are in some way or who is better liked can make us feel inferior. The feeling of having transgressed also provokes negative attitudes toward ourselves. The sense of goodness that is inherent in each of us incites us to feel shame when we do not measure up to what we conceive is good.

There are a number of ways in which we can we come to feel that we have worth. We can find someone who accepts us and let that acceptance soak in. (Often, all that we need for this is just one person.) We can work on realizing that God values us even though we are not as talented as others or even though we are not as successful as we would like to be. We can also work on accepting God's forgiveness.

These ways of coming to feel that we have worth require work and struggle, because we do not overcome the sources of our negative feelings about ourselves instantaneously. We do not simply accept God's acceptance of us and then feel good the rest of our lives without a pang of self-hate. Part of our lifelong journey of faith is letting God's affirmation of us sink more and more deeply into us.

> **It is not pride to regard ourselves as having worth, but true assessment.**

LOVING OURSELVES AS WE LOVE OUR NEIGHBORS

It is extremely repugnant to love someone who has done something of which we strongly disapprove. If we were to find out that a married acquaintance has committed adultery, our first reaction would be dismay or strong revulsion. If we were to discover that a friend regularly gets drunk, our opinion of her would change drastically.

One circumstance that makes it easier to accept such persons is the realization that we ourselves are in the same category, both because of what we have done and because of what our inner lives contain—the thoughts, desires, and fantasies from which others would recoil if they knew of them. We hide these from others because we are not sure that they would accept us if they knew about them. We also hide these from ourselves, because we could not accept ourselves if we explicitly acknowledged them. This fact indicates that we do not accept ourselves in spite of what we disapprove of about ourselves, but because of our admirable features—the good we do, the special virtues we believe we possess, our achievements, and our status in comparison to others.

The love that God has for us, which is an "in spite of" love and not a "because of" love, is what he wants us to have toward others. Though we may find it difficult to engage in this kind of love, we readily agree that we should. It does not so readily occur to us that we can love ourselves in the same way. We find it even harder to love ourselves in this way than we do others. We tend to be more critical of ourselves and less accepting of our true worth. Yet God wants us to love ourselves with the "in spite of" love that he has toward us.

> **The second great commandment, "You shall love your neighbor as yourself," means that we should love our neighbor as we ought to love ourselves. The reverse is just as true—we should love ourselves as we ought to love our neighbor.**

THE EFFECTS OF LOVING AND BEING LOVED

Søren Kierkegaard has a marvelous paragraph on the biblical affirmation, "Love covers a multitude of sins" (1 Pt 4:8). He writes,

> With respect to sin . . . , there are no constraining conditions so rehabilitating as love. How frequently anger, smoldering within, only waiting for an occasion, how frequently it has been smothered because love gave no occasion! How frequently evil desire, watching and waiting for an occasion in the sensual anxiety of curiosity, how often it has perished in birth because love gave no occasion at all and lovingly watched lest any occasion at all be given! How often resentment in the soul has been stilled, resentment which was so assured and so prepared, yes, so poised to find yet a new occasion to be wronged by the world, by men, by God, by everything, how often it has been stilled into a quieter mood because love gave no occasion to be wronged at all. How frequently this conceited and defiant attitude passed away . . . because love, so alleviating, so mildly dispersive, gave no occasion at all to the sick imagination! . . . O, how many crimes have been prevented, how many evil enterprises brought to naught, how many desperate resolutions drawn into forgetfulness, how many sinful thoughts halted on the way to becoming acts, how many unconsidered words stifled in time, because love gave no occasion![17]

Kierkegaard is saying that when we love people, all kinds of undesirable attitudes, emotions, and desires are pushed out. Anger, evil desire, resentment, conceit, and a defiant attitude are all smothered by love. It makes these states "perish," causes them to be "stilled," so that they "pass away." Love "constrains and rehabilitates" and as a result anger, evil desire, and resentment are prevented, brought to naught, forgotten, halted, stifled.

If love pushes out these undesirable states in other people, then it also pushes them out in us when we are loved. When we are loved, our anger, evil desires, resentments, conceits, and defiant attitudes are smothered. They recede because love replaces them. We no longer need to be resentful or have conceit. Being loved makes them lose their hold on us.

There is another fact about what love does that Kierkegaard doesn't mention—love constrains and rehabilitates the one who gives it as well as the one who receives it. Giving love has the same effects on the giver as receiving love has on the receiver. When we love, our resentments are displaced, our conceit gets smothered, and our evil desires are forgotten.

> **We need to be loved not only because we need the love but also because we need the restoration it evokes.**

SPIRITUAL COURAGE

Courage does not seem to be a particularly important virtue in everyday life. It appears to be relevant more for those in war or in some heroic adventure, but not for daily concerns. It seems remote and inapplicable to the things we ordinarily do.

Yet there are several features of the life of faith that require a good deal of courage. One of them is loving. Loving is often risky and a bit scary. We instinctively feel it to be dangerous, partly because we cannot always predict what will happen to the one loved, but also partly because of what we vaguely sense will happen to us. We will become different. We will have to venture forth from our comfortable self-centeredness. We will have to move away from places with which we are so familiar that departing from them feels a little like leaving home. Loving extravagantly is a fearful thing.

A second feature of the life of faith that requires courage is facing ourselves. To live a larger life, we need to gaze inward to find out what we are really like. The very prospect of doing so, however, is fearful, for we might find that our lives are built on sinking sand. We might find malice or envy. We might find that we are not sure what the point of our lives is or that we are failures.

Much of what we do in life is designed to flee from self-knowledge: we lose ourselves in activities or in other people so we can avoid having to look inside ourselves. The easiest path is to refuse to look at our feelings and passions, so that we do not have to admit that we possess envy, lust, or impulses of self-glorification. Long stretches of time go by without our asking who we are and what we are doing with our lives.

A third feature of the life of faith that requires courage is letting ourselves be overtaken by God's love. God's love is fiery, for accepting it means that we have to give up our dearest schemes of self-justification. We have to accept the fact that God loves us no matter what. This requires courage, for God's love, when fully accepted, makes us new all the way through, and we are intensely afraid to give up our old habits and desires. To do so, we must overcome the fear that we will never again be able to indulge ourselves in them.

Though the courage to maintain one's values in the face of opposition is part of the life of faith, it is not the same courage that is involved in loving, obtaining self-knowledge, and accepting God's love.

The truest courage overcomes inner fears.

SEVEN

LIVING BY GRACE

For years Paul's admonition to "work out our own salvation" (Phil 2:12) was incomprehensible to me. It sounded as if he was advocating a save-yourself-by-your-good-works doctrine, which would conflict with what he says elsewhere about the necessity of faith. I could not imagine what else he might have meant.

Now it seems obvious to me that he meant something like, "Let your faith be evident in what you do" or "Live as though you have faith." It would be as if a commencement speaker were to admonish the graduates to whom he was speaking, "Now go out and live what you have learned."

This is what I want to say about grace. Not only is grace essential to the existence of faith, it is central to the way we live our faith. The pivotal realities in a faith-lived life are grace-related. Envy and lust for admiration, for example, need to be undercut, and the only way to do so is with grace. Living with a spouse or being part of a community of believers requires both giving and receiving grace. The power of the fat, relentless ego can be blunted only with a plentiful amount of grace.

WHERE IS GRACE?

Paul says two things about grace: "By grace you have been saved" (Eph 2:8) and "It is well for the heart to be strengthened by grace" (Heb 13:9).

These two declarations indicate that grace both gets us started on the life of faith and is significant to the way we live it. When one observes communities of faith, however, one notices that it is sometimes difficult to detect grace being exhibited in interactions among their members.

Why is this so? Perhaps the answer is that self-justification remains even in those who are overtly committed to faith. Self-justification is that in us that makes us want to say, "You need to be this way or to do that," and to add unconsciously, "to be acceptable to God." It is the thing in us that makes us emphasize the "you"—the congregation, the audience, other believers—anyone but ourselves. It makes us adopt high standards as to what people need to do in order to be approved by God.

In our everyday interactions, too, there seems to be little giving of grace. The very institution in which one would expect grace to be most evident—the Christian church—sometimes contains just the opposite of grace. Put less harshly, self-justification is mixed in with grace, and we scarcely notice this fact because self-justification also blinds us to its presence.

The plain truth is that even if we believe in grace, we still feel the need to impress others with our goodness, knowledge, subtle insights, and admirable qualities. Thus, self-justification affects us even though we officially believe in grace.

Perhaps the rock bottom fact here is that the most difficult thing in life is to receive and give grace. It is for me. I therefore turn my observations into a lament, both for Christian institutions and for myself.

The solution is not to distance ourselves from the problem as if it is someone else's and to think that we are better than they are because they have a problem and we don't. It is to look for grace, actively to seek it out, for, to reverse what I said earlier, it is there, mixed in with self-justification. Part of the solution, also, is to create grace, that is, to be bearers of it to others.

Religious communities both convey the love of God to us and shield us from it.

GIVING GRACE

An ideal community of faith, whether it be a formal institution or an informal gathering, is one in which the giving of grace to others in the community is a prominent feature. This means that those in the community make a conscious effort to give grace. Doing so is a conspicuous characteristic of the community and not just something that its members take for granted. The people in the community go out of their way to give grace, seizing opportunities that come to them.

What they give is a replica of the grace that God gives us—an acceptance that does not depend on what we do.

Those to whom they give grace are other acquaintances in the community, and not just those who they think have a special need, such as those who are not liked very much or those who are marginally connected with the group. We often think that we need to have a grace-attitude toward people with special needs. My point here is that, though this is true, we should have a grace-attitude toward everyone in a community as a matter of course.

This grace-attitude differs from the attitude of granting acceptance to others on the basis of what they do. Standards of performance are not paramount in our connections with them. It also differs from the attitude of indifference toward others.

Why should we give grace to others in a community of faith? We should do so because they need it. They need to feel acceptance, and we can give them this. They need to sense that they are loved, and we can be the ones through whom they come to have this sense.

In addition, our connection to God is often tied to the way in which we are connected to other people. If we adopt a standard-of-performance way of connecting to people, then that is likely to be the way we connect to God. If we are indifferent toward others, we are likely to be indifferent toward God, but if we have a grace-attitude toward people, more than likely we will connect to God in a grace-way. (Each of these works the other way as well.)

Lastly, we ourselves want to be recipients of a grace-attitude. It is, in fact, something we long for. Most of us are desperate for a community in which grace is prominent; we are grace-starved.

There is a different answer to this question of why we should give grace to others in a community of faith. If we have been given grace by God, it will spill over naturally and spontaneously. We will become the kind of person who does not base acceptability simply on performance, who is not indifferent to others, and who intensely desires to give grace.

How can we give grace? We can touch people on the shoulder, give them praise, and listen attentively to them. We can work on becoming kind and gracious. We can be affirming and encouraging.

> When we give grace we will be given it in return, but we cannot give grace in order to get it, for then it ceases to be grace.

ACCEPTING OTHERS

Why is it so hard to accept other people as they are? Perhaps one reason is that we want them to be like us. We are afraid of differences. Also, we want others to live the way we think it is right to live and to believe what we think is true. We judge them when they do not. This is particularly true of their political, moral, and religious beliefs. In addition, envy may be working in us to set up barriers. It may also be that we do not feel accepted by anyone, so that we do not have anything in us to give to others.

Is it desirable to be accepting? The best answer is to ask ourselves, Do we want to be accepted? Do we want others to shun us because we dress differently or have a different hair style? Would we like it if others rejected us because we expressed doubts, had different beliefs, or fell into sin?

What is acceptance? It is not the same as liking people, nor is it the same as approving of their behavior or beliefs. It does involve acting agreeably toward people even though we disapprove of what they do. It often means not saying anything about what we disapprove of. It also involves making efforts to understand. When we accept someone, we can say, "I take you as you are." Our attitude is, "The other person is okay as she is and we do not try to change her. We do not let her imperfections get in the way."

How can we be more accepting? We can come to possess an inner security, so that we do not feel threatened when others differ from us. We can realize that we want others to accept us, so that we can give to them what we want them to give to us. We can be conscious of the fact that God loves them, so that we can have the same stance toward them as God has. We can be aware of the fact that God loves us, so that we can give away some of what we have received.

> Often it is less our words and more our demeanor that conveys acceptance.

LIVING BY GRACE

Søren Kierkegaard once noted the disparity between our Sunday talk about faith, genuine though it may be, and our experience of it during the week.

> Last Sunday . . . the clergyman said that a human being can do absolutely nothing of himself, and we all understood it. . . . Even the most religious man will have occasion to catch himself a dozen times a day entertaining the delusion that he can at least do something.[18]

When I examine my own experience of the reality of God's grace (with more honesty than I customarily possess), I find that it is present only occasionally. There are several reasons for this. I am busy, both physically and mentally, and am constantly doing something or thinking about something. No doubt this reason has a certain legitimacy, for one can hardly be experiencing grace when concentrating on a task. Yet I find that I use this busyness as a distraction to avoid experiencing grace.

In addition, I have long thought of the life of faith as consisting predominantly of doing things—virtuous things, things pleasing to God—and not principally as a deepening of the experience of grace. I also find in myself nearly irresistible impulses of self-justification and out-of-control self-centeredness.

Kierkegaard's observation suggests that the experience of God's grace is not just something to understand, but is integral to a life of genuine faith. If I were to "live by grace," I would have a consciousness of God's grace during many moments of the day. The impelling force of my life would be to be aware of that grace, to let it dominate my thoughts, and to allow it to push out alien instincts. My desires for approval, success, and others' esteem would not move me as much as they now do, and neither would the drive to compare myself favorably to others. My schemes of self-justification would lose most of their hold on me. I would not conceive of my identity in terms of my successes and approvals, but in terms of grace. My single passion would be to possess grace, to feel it, to let it direct my motives, to let it sink into the deepest parts of myself. My aim in life would be to be so thoroughly permeated by grace that my hidden parts would not secretly pursue success and approval and others' high esteem.

When we live by grace, our defenses crumble. The barriers we erect to prevent God from knowing our secrets, the fronts we build so people will see how good we are, are shattered. We feel naked before God, with nothing to hide behind. We feel, too, that we cannot escape, for that is our first impulse—to get up and run away—but we also feel drawn to this grace, for though its purging power is painful, it gives relief from the oppression of guilt and inner dividedness. We feel that God accepts us in spite of our waywardness. This feeling takes hold of us and captivates the center of our consciousness.

When we live by grace, we discover that although our experience of it may have been superficial at first, it infuses itself into us more deeply as we go through our days. We find that we can experience grace even when we are going about everyday affairs, at odd moments during the day and not just when we are programmed to experience it, such as during church services or times of quiet meditation. We find that grace gives a rest and a peace that contrasts markedly with our anxious quest for meaning.

Grace changes us into the kind of person we had no inkling of being.

GRACE AND SELF-JUSTIFICATION

One of the things that undermines our experience of grace most is self-justification. "Justification" means "being acceptable to God" and "self-justification" means doing something to make ourselves acceptable to God. Self-justification is antithetical to the experience of grace, for grace means that God makes us acceptable to him: he accepts us in spite of our shortfalls.

We engage in self-justification in numerous ways. Our jobs are a strong source of self-justification, especially for those of us who are professionals, because we are acutely conscious that our jobs are held in high esteem. The houses in which we live are a source of self-justification, and so are the clothes we wear. We also use our accomplishments as a means of making ourselves acceptable, and we use sex, sex appeal, and our looks, which we believe others admire. Knowing certain important people can also be used in a self-justifying way, as can the fact that we are well-liked, or the mere fact that we have friends. We are conscious of our position in society—that we are not on the bottom, poor, dirty, with second-class possessions—and this makes us feel a cosmic acceptability.

We engage in self-justification in religious ways as well. We sometimes think of ourselves as being admired for being spiritual or for doing good, religious things. We feel accepted by our community of faith when we conform to its patterns of acting and ways of talking. We know that others of like mind approve of us when we believe the right things.

Our drive to engage in self-justification may be the strongest drive we possess. We can scarcely help ourselves sometimes—we find ourselves almost automatically doing and thinking things because of it. There is hardly an activity that escapes it. Moreover, and this is the scariest part, we often engage in it without knowing that we do. We can go for years, decades even, and suddenly wake up with surprise and sorrow—"I've been using that just to justify myself." It is no wonder that our experiences of grace are so intermittent.

What is the remedy? One is to root around underneath our surface motives until we find the hidden impulses we use to justify ourselves. Another is to pray the tax collector's prayer, "God, have mercy on me," not just once, but twice, more even, until it soaks in.

> Being open to grace involves letting go of some of our dearest cravings.

ADMIRATION AND GRACE

Many of us have a strong impulse to be admired. The impulse to be admired is different from the need for acceptance and love. Admiration says, "Look how good I am at doing this" and "Do you see how I am better than other people?"

The intensity of the impulse to be admired can be gauged by noticing the lengths to which we go, the degree to which we subject ourselves to pain, and the amount we go out of our way so that we can obtain admiration. By these criteria, the intensity is very high. We desperately want to be noticed. If a day goes by without episodes of admiration, we feel diminished. If there were no admiration in our lives, we would shrivel up and die.

The impulse gets played out in a wide variety of ways—in the clothes we wear, our hair styles, the clever things we say, the accolades we obtain from our superiors, the games we win. There is nothing we cannot turn into a means of being admired.

One of the results of the impulse to be admired is that it provokes us to admire ourselves. This self-admiration and the admiration we get from others get mixed up in us into one giant morass, so that we can scarcely distinguish one from the other.

The impulse to be admired is, of course, the opposite of being open to God's grace. To be open to grace we must set aside our desire to be big; we must root out our craving to be better than others. Openness to grace is acceptance of God's acceptance; it is allowing ourselves to be loved by someone who is not impressed with our schemes to make ourselves admirable.

Because the impulse to be admired is so strong, the life of faith involves a struggle between it and being open to grace. Sometimes the conflict gets fierce, sometimes we succumb to admiration, but sometimes we feel the grace in spite of the desire to be admired.

Graciously accepting praise is one thing; seeking admiration to expand our egos is another. Grace undercuts the latter and enables us to do the former.

ENVY AND GRACE

The dictionary defines envy as "a painful or resentful awareness of an advantage enjoyed by another conjoined with a desire to possess the same advantage." Envy must be distinguished from jealousy, which occurs when one is "intolerant of rivalry or unfaithfulness." The typical case of jealousy occurs when one person is jealous because another person is perceived to be a rival in love. Envy, however, occurs without this kind of rivalry. Envy must also be distinguished from covetousness, which is the inordinate "desire for what belongs to another." Simply coveting what others have is not the same as the resentfulness in envy.

A variety of advantages provoke envy. We may want to be known as a good athlete or a good teacher. We may want to be a public speaker or singer, or want to look better than we do, or be smart and be able to say perceptive things. If we resent others who are better than we are in any of these ways, we possess envy.

The extent to which envy pervades our lives is probably a good deal larger than we suspect, and the intensity of our envy is probably sharper than we are aware. We have a strong impulse to be better than others in some way. If we could concede the truth about ourselves, we would have to admit that we want to be the best in the world.

Envy is not without effect on how we connect to others. Because of envy, we tend not to praise others for their accomplishments. (Is there anything that is harder than to praise another?) We are more likely to criticize and are less likely to love. (Can we admire those we envy?)

Why do we feel resentment when we notice that someone has an advantage? The answer is that we feel diminished by the fact that the other person possesses the advantage. We feel that the accomplishment or native quality of the other casts a negative light on us. Although the other's accomplishment or quality does not actually make us inferior, we feel that it does.

What causes us to feel diminished when we notice another person's accomplishment? The reason we do so is that we want to be looked up to in the same way the other person is looked up to. We feel inadequate and unaccepted; we possess a sense of not being good enough, so we resent the fact that someone else has something that would make us feel adequate and accepted if we had it.

At bottom, what underlies envy is our desire to justify our existence. We want to feel valuable and to compensate for inadequacies or failure. These are spiritual categories, for they spring from our need to feel right before God.

The solution to envy, therefore, is to accept God's grace. When we feel that God accepts us, the urge to be envious dissipates. God tells us that he forgives us and that we are acceptable to him. As a result, we do not feel diminished by others' advantages. They are, in fact, no longer thought of as advantages.

When we receive God's grace, we can admire others' abilities and accomplishments, even though we know we will never have them. We can tell people that we like what they do. We can encourage them and love them and touch them, without feeling uneasy when we are in their presence. We come to feel secure, so that we do not constantly need to compensate for perceived inferiority. Resentment no longer nags us, and we become free.

Envy is deadly because it disconnects us from grace.

ADDICTIONS

When we think of addictions, we normally think of smoking, drinking, and using drugs. There are other addictions that are not so commonly recognized: coffee drinking, television watching, sexual activity, overeating, and buying. In addition, there are inner states to which we can become addicted. Among these are having critical thoughts, envy, hating ourselves, admiring ourselves, thinking of ourselves as superior to others, using other people simply to satisfy our needs, justifying our existence by our successes, coveting others' possessions, and letting their disapproval govern our lives.

Addictions have three features:

The first is that we find it hard to stop them. If we tried, we could not easily do so. We are controlled by the addictionæthis is as true of admiring ourselves as it is of coffee drinking or smoking. If we are addicted to admiring ourselves, we cannot stop any more easily than if we are addicted to a morning cup of coffee.

The second feature is that each is a habit that is done automatically, without consciously choosing it. Again, this is as true of envy as it is of addictive television watching. Without thinking of what we are doing, we turn on the television, or resent another's successes, or say critical things without provocation.

The third feature of addictions is that they fill voids in our lives. We would feel that something were missing if we did not engage in the addictive activity or possess the addictive inner state. The activity or inner state is like a friend that eases our loneliness; it may make us feel important and raise low self-esteem; it may block the pain of feeling unloved or make us feel as if life is okay. If we are addicted to certain sorts of sexual activity or to justifying our existence by public successes, the thought of eliminating them feels like eliminating something we dearly need.

We may pride ourselves on being free from addictions, but the truth is that we can possess inner addictions even though we are free from outer addictions. The inner ones, in fact, are even more uncontrollable, because they involve needs that go deep into the human condition. Because we so desperately need to feel justified, we easily get into the habit of having critical thoughts, being envious, and admiring ourselves. Pretty soon, the habit controls us without our knowing that it does so.

Three things can help us deal with these addictions:

The first is to become conscious of them. We need to become aware of what we habitually use to fill the voids in our lives, for the habit is not likely to go away by itself. It needs to be fought. Being aware of the addiction, however, is not enough, for we may be aware of our self-admiration and bask in it anyway, just as we may be aware of indulging in potato chips and cookies but still be unable to stop.

We also need, secondly, to confess, to admit with sorrow, regret, and distaste, that we have the addiction. We need to develop an aversion that can overpower the inclination in the habit.

An aversion, too, is not enough, for we need, thirdly, to fill the voids in us, so that we do not feel the need for the addictive feelings and thought patterns. With the voids filled, the automatic inclination to hate ourselves or to use others merely as a means to satiate ourselves declines. When, for example, we accept God's love, we do not feel so strongly the need to use others for our own ends or to justify ourselves by their admiration.

Because of the power of inner addictions, we cannot be free from them instantaneously. One essential element of the life of faith is the ongoing and unwavering effort to free ourselves from them.

> Addictions start with desires, which become habits, then uncontrollable activities or attitudes. Love is voluntary from start to end.

ACCEPTANCE OR KNOWLEDGE?

There are two kinds of faith communities: one in which there is a high degree of caring and acceptance, and one in which there is a high degree of knowledge about the faith itself.

In the first kind of community, people are accepted no matter what their viewpoints are and no matter how they live. There is respect for the fact that people are at various stages in their spiritual growth and for the fact that people are different. People feel free to be themselves and to grow in ways of their own choosing. They do not need to be defensive or fake or put on masks. Because of these characteristics, this kind of community usually has a measure of doctrinal and lifestyle diversity.

This first kind of faith community exemplifies several biblical admonitions: "Do not judge others, so that God will not judge you" (Mt 7:1), "Be tolerant with one another" (Col 3:13), and "Show a gentle attitude toward everyone" (Phil 4:5).

In the second kind of faith community, there is more of an emphasis on knowing the content of the faith. Sermons are frequently designed with that aim, and so are religious education sessions. Right beliefs are held in high regard, doctrine is discussed, books by theologians are read, and knowledge of traditional beliefs is respected. Because of the importance placed on knowing in this second kind of community, it usually has less doctrinal and lifestyle diversity than the first kind.

Although both acceptance and knowledge are desirable, it is difficult to combine them. If there is a great deal of acceptance, those who are different will feel welcome, but those who want conformity to doctrine will be uneasy, perhaps disgruntled. If there is an emphasis on knowing doctrine, then there is likely to be an emphasis on conformity to it, so that those who do not will not feel welcome. In either case, there probably will be tension.

The question we need to ask is, How can we retain the good features of both kinds of faith communities? Because it is hard to do this, we also have to ask, If we had to choose between the two, which would we choose?

We seldom find a faith community that meets all our expectations—and just as seldom find a perfect person.

THE AWE-EVOKING CHARACTER OF GRACE

Half a dozen times during the past fifteen years, I have lain in the grass on a summer evening and observed the stars. On a couple of these occasions, when the sky was filled to the brim with those tiny points of light, I have been overtaken with a sense of the immensity of the universe. My mind has reeled, and I have had to put the thought of that immensity from it.

I like to visit Lake Michigan and listen to the waves. When I am in a meditative mood, I say to myself, "God knows the location of each molecule in this splash" (if I happen to be sitting on a boulder). "And not only that, he knows the location of each molecule in every other splash on this strip of boulders. And he can predict the location of each molecule in all these splashes just before they occur." It is not long before my mind staggers. I can take that feeling for only a few seconds.

Sometimes on my way to my office in the morning I walk past a pond. I often stop for half a minute to observe it. Now and then the air is so motionless that one can count the leaves of the trees reflected on the surface of the still water. "What beauty!" I have exclaimed to myself. On these occasions, my mind has quickly taken me to the thought that the whole universe possesses the same beauty of this single, precise reflection. Again, my mind reels, and I have had to turn away from the scene and trudge to my office.

Now I come to grace. Two or three times in my life—not much more often than that—I have had this thought: "We are a fallen race. We live on a planet with a cloud over it; we are a blight on the universe. I am a member of that race, and am fallen like the rest. We do not deserve to be loved, yet grace accepts us—me—anyway." This thought has turned into a feeling—a feeling that is as intense as the awareness of the universe's immensity, as forceful as the consciousness of the infinitude of God's knowledge, and as overwhelming as the perception of the beauty. It is not my mind, however, that staggers and reels; it is my heart that nearly explodes.

Feeling the magnificence of grace is as rare as it is wonderful.

EIGHT

NEVER THE SAME AGAIN

One of the most powerful questions is "How can I become different?" This is a "mover" question. It moves us to imagine new ways we can love; it makes us think of virtues we can work on; it drags us out of our complacency. We cannot ask it without in some way being drawn to something new.

One of the features of the life of faith is this sense of being drawn to something new. We find ourselves wanting to develop new patterns of living and to connect to people in fresh ways. We also find ourselves wondering how there could have been a time when we were not attracted to these. We possess sadness and regret that we once had little or no interest in matters of significance. What has happened is that an irrevocable change has taken place in us.

This, of course, is not quite true, for our desire for newness often fades and we sometimes lose the sense of being drawn to God. It is true enough, though—enough, that is, to move us toward constant renewal.

THE BARREN TREE

Brother Lawrence, a seventeenth-century French monk, was converted when he encountered a bare tree one winter day. Here is an account of his conversion as told to a friend.

> The first time I saw Brother Lawrence was upon the third of August, 1666. He told me that God had done him a singular favor in his conversion at the age of eighteen.
>
> That in the winter, seeing a tree stripped of its leaves, and considering that within a little time the leaves would be renewed, and after that the flowers and fruit appear, he received a high view of the providence and power of God, which has never since been effaced from his soul. That this view had perfectly set him loose from the world, and kindled in him such a love for God that he could not tell whether it had increased during the more than forty years he had lived since.[19]

One thing that this account tells us is that conversion experiences can happen anywhere. They can happen when one is listening to a minister preach, while reading a book, writing in one's journal, or meditating in a quiet place. They can happen during an altar call, while lying on a couch, or when reading the Bible by oneself. They can even happen while riding a motorcycle, as it did for Alan Davis. Alan was suddenly overwhelmed by God's presence one afternoon when he was out on his motorcycle. For nearly an hour more he continued riding, singing as he rode.

Another thing that this account tells us is that almost anything can awaken in us the desire to have a new heart: the sight of a fat bud or an unfolding flower, observing someone praying alone in a public place, listening to someone recount her conversion.

The very thought of leaves springing from spare branches prompts me to ask, "Why don't I become new, too? Why don't I leave behind my fear of loving, my addictions, my attachment to ego expansion? Why don't I become more open to God's love, let go of the old, and let myself be revitalized?"

Part of us wants renewal now, but part wants to wait until some later day.

IMAGINING NEW POSSIBILITIES

One of the prominent themes in nearly every conception of spirituality is the idea of becoming new. In the Bible this idea is embodied in the notion of being a "new creature" and in the injunction that we are to "be transformed by the renewing of our minds." We are told even that we need to be born all over again.

How does this happen? How do we become new?

One answer that a theologian is likely to give is that God makes us new. At the same time, there is a sense in which we are active participants in working out this newness. There are specific attitudes we can adopt and specific activities in which we can engage to deepen our renewal.

One of these is simply to imagine ourselves being new. By this I mean imagining ourselves being different, picturing to ourselves new ways of acting and new ways of feeling.

Here are some examples:

We can imagine ourselves talking with people in gentle ways or exhibiting interest in what they say by our facial expressions. We can picture ourselves carrying bags of food to a shelter and interacting with the homeless people there.

The fascinating thing about picturing ourselves loving in new ways is that doing so has a certain drawing power. Something about these pictures in our minds impels us actually to love in the ways we imagine.

Most of the time, though, our imaginations are occupied with other matters, such as music, sports, and travel. With but a fraction of the effort we expend on these we could picture ourselves exhibiting virtues in new ways or taking on new patterns of living. The result would be that we would become different in ways in which we had hitherto never thought.

Imagination has a double power: it can trick us into thinking we are something we are not and it can draw us into new prospects.

REDISCOVERING THE RESURRECTION

Many of us who have grown up going to church take the resurrection of Jesus almost for granted. We have not come to it from an initial state of disbelief or skepticism. This state, however, is our natural reaction to reports of unusual occurrences. We would, for example, be skeptical if we were told that someone in the weight room of a health club had lifted 300 pounds with one arm, and we would be positively disbelieving if we heard that someone could make objects disappear. The resurrection is like these, and if it had not been for our church life, we probably would have been very skeptical upon first hearing of it.

The first people to hear about the resurrection had this attitude. The women who were told by the angels that Jesus was not in the tomb were puzzled, and Peter and John had to go to the tomb to see for themselves that it was empty.

What would our own reaction be upon becoming convinced that Jesus really did come back to life? Perhaps our first reaction would be one of astonishment—something impossible has happened. Our second reaction might be that something beyond the human has taken place, and more particularly, that God has come crashing into our realm. We might even feel that God has come crashing into our own lives.

God does, to be sure, lure us gently with his patient love, but in the resurrection, he appears to be employing the opposite strategy. It is as if he has used an explosion to shake us loose from our old ways and to turn us around.

Sometimes we have to rediscover old truths in order to keep them fresh.

NEVER THE SAME AGAIN

In her simple but captivating poem "Bethlehem," Maura Eichner vividly displays what happens when we meet the Food that gives eternal life.

> Bethlehem
> We stand at a simple table
> and take bread warmed between candle flame.
> It is we who are taken.
> After this food we can never be the same.[20]

There is something captivating about the One whom we encounter at a Table. We are attracted to this person and are taken by him.

A number of qualities draw us to him. "Bethlehem" mentions one: "We stand at a *simple* table." We meet not power but lowliness, not riches but poverty, not self-exaltation but giving.

Other qualities draw us as well. When we see God's purity, we find ourselves wanting both it and forgiveness. When we experience God's love, we find ourselves wanting to savor it and to extend it to others. A number of feelings overtake us—a feeling of being at peace with ourselves, of being accepted, of gratitude. We find ourselves, too, unable to return to our pre-encounter self. We cannot be the same again.

Once we have tasted the new, we cannot go back to the old.

STAYING SPIRITUALLY FRESH

Some years ago I attended an academic conference in Provo, Utah, about seventy miles south of Salt Lake City. I had vaguely known that there were mountains in the area, but did not see any coming in on the plane or driving to Provo, since it was dark. The next morning when I drew back the curtains in the motel room, I gasped at the sight of a snow-covered mountain whose base was not more than a mile away. It filled nearly the whole window.

My initial feelings were exhilaration and awe. I stood at the window for some minutes, taking in the scene bit by bit. Its largeness and beauty were too much to absorb all at once. When I could move again, I did so with a certain abstractness.

It was the same throughout the day and a half I was at the conference. I stood on street corners gazing at the mountain. I paid little attention to sidewalks as I walked toward the mountain. After a meeting, I moved to a window to obtain another fill.

Now, years later, this memory, though pleasant, is dim. Rarely do I even recall the scene. On occasion, I sense that I have lost something. The initial exhilaration has worn off entirely.

The life of faith is the same. In our periodic highs, we are overcome by love and elated by hope. These feelings last for a few hours, perhaps even for a day or two, but they fade, and the memory of them flits in and out of our minds. We become absorbed in work and home activities, or we succumb to weariness. Our daily duties numb us. Time passes and we experience another high, but again the good feelings diminish and become extinct.

How, then, can we stay spiritually fresh all the time?

The first point to make is that the question may be wrong. The truth is not only that we cannot be high all the time but that we should not expect to be. A life of faith does not consist of being high every moment. It contains a fair amount of strenuous work and a great deal of evenhanded calm. Moreover, spiritual freshness is not always, or hardly ever, being high. It consists largely of readiness and openness and awareness.

Yet we certainly can be fresh more than we normally are. Perhaps the question to ask is, What can we do to keep ourselves from going stale?

Of the many answers we can give to this question, I want to suggest one: Stay aware of our inner condition. Most of the time we become indifferent and numb without our even knowing that we are.

> ## Staying fresh is as difficult as going numb is easy.

SPIRITUAL ADVENTURE

At times during our lives, we want to go on adventures, do something new and different and get a little excitement. We become tired of doing the same old things and feel the need for some kind of adventure to rejuvenate a tired and worn-out life. To be sure, we need discipline, habit, and regular patterns, but we need freshness as well.

What are some of the features of adventure? Newness is one and so is excitement. Risk is another, for often in an adventure we do not know exactly what we are getting ourselves into, and danger may be present. Creativity is also a characteristic of adventure, for we must create the newness or it will not seem like *our* adventure.

Adventure brings renewal and invigoration, a sense that everything is new, and a certain brightness in our emotions. Some of our old patterns may be upset, or they may become tolerable again or obtain new meaning.

Why not spiritual adventure as well? Living spiritually does, indeed, involve discipline, habits, and regular patterns, but these may become mechanical, as any habit can, and we may find ourselves in a tired rut, in the "habit of piety," as Graham Greene put it in *The Power and the Glory*.

Spiritual adventure involves the same features that everyday adventure involves: newness and excitement, risk, creativity, and sometimes danger. The results are the same as well: our spirituality becomes fresh, we acquire a brightness in our faith, and our habits spring from an overflowing spontaneity.

Most of our everyday activities can be turned into adventures: simple love of a friend or love of someone who is ugly or unlovable in some way or who is difficult to get along with. Regarding these as adventures instead of as duties will turn ourselves into something new.

The greatest adventures take place inside us.

GLIMPSES OF HEAVEN

During rare moments, we obtain brief glimpses of what heaven will be like. Our experiences on these occasions are so intense and wonderful that we do not want to return to the struggles, drudgery, weariness, tears, and inner turmoil of our daily existence. But we have to return. We cannot sustain the intensity of the experiences for long.

Sometimes glimpses of heaven come to us unexpectedly; other times we can induce them by meditating in a peaceful location. They can come to us when we are sitting beside a lake listening to the waves, or when we are by ourselves in our rooms, or even when we are surrounded by people in a restaurant or meeting. Sometimes they occur after we have participated in a particularly meaningful situation.

If our glimpses are intense, we will remember them for a long time—the location, the surroundings, and the feelings and thoughts we had. The effects, too, will be numerous. We might feel frustration that real life is so different, sorrow that we do not possess what we glimpse, a feeling of tragedy about our pre-heaven state, and contrition for our shortfall. The glimpses can also convey to us a sense of completeness, of being filled with God's love and peace, a calm amidst turbulence, and at the same time leave us with a longing for something more than what we ordinarily possess. They can produce in us an impulse to exemplify what we glimpse, a dream of what we really want in life, and a deep-felt conviction that life is worth living.

Heaven frequently feels vague and distant; it is this life that entrances us.

GOD'S CLOWNS

The chapel speaker was a clown. He wasn't dressed as a clown while he was speaking to us, but he was dressed as one, he told us, the afternoon he took a group of ministers to a shopping mall to illustrate to them what it is like to live with faith in an unfaithful world. The ministers were also dressed as clowns.

Their activity at the mall was simply to walk around blowing bubbles. They had made a solemn pact before leaving that under no circumstances would any of them say anything.

The clowns attracted a great deal of attention. As they spread around the mall, clusters of onlookers formed around each of them. Children laughed. Adults chuckled. A despondent old man set aside his cares for a moment.

Unfortunately, not everyone reacted in these ways. Some adults wondered what was going on. The clowns, bound by their pact of silence, did not explain. Others remarked that the spectacle of bubble-blowing clowns wandering about a shopping mall was a bit silly.

Some of the store managers became concerned. They asked the clowns why they were there. In response, the clowns sent clouds of bubbles skyward, to the great delight of giggling children. When the mall superintendent requested that the clowns leave, he, too, was answered with broad smiles and clouds of bubbles. That, of course, could not be tolerated.

The police were called, but their luck was no better. They were finally forced to round up all the clowns, march them single file to the paddy wagon, and take them to the police station.

Doing that, however, did not help matters. Although the clowns had had their bubble-blowing equipment taken away, they still had one weapon left—enormous, silent smiles. And they used that weapon in response to the police chief's insistent questioning.

No doubt the situation would have deteriorated further had not the chief clown—our chapel speaker—finally explained the matter. The clowns were released, but with a warning: "Don't do it again."

"Now," said the chapel speaker, "there are three features of this experience that resemble what it is like for people of faith to live in a secular society: the clowns created joy, people thought they were crazy, and they got into trouble."

People of faith create joy. They ease the burden of care and lighten the load of guilt. They befriend the lonely, respect the rights of the oppressed, and resolve antagonisms. They heal the sick, share with the poor, and love the unlovely.

Sometimes this joy is temporary; other times it is longer lasting. Children laugh. Grandparents smile. The poor cease worrying and enemies shake hands. The guilty are forgiven and broken lives are restored.

Unfortunately, not everyone esteems those who create joy. People who are molded by secular values sometimes look upon people of faith as quaint, odd, and even a bit crazy. Who in her right mind would resign from a high-paying job to serve the needs of society's outcasts? What sane person would deliberately give away her money instead of buying in-style clothes? Why would anyone want to waste time singing songs on a sunny Sunday summer morning?

In a world molded by secular values, people with faith will, from time to time, be resented. If not, something may be wrong. They may have adopted lifestyles too much like those of secular society, or their faith may not be so clear and definite as to be noticed. But if it is clear and definite, they can expect resistance.

Sometimes resistance will be relatively mild ridicule, criticism, or pressure to conform to other values. Other times it will be harsher, perhaps threats for befriending a member of a different race or harassment by coworkers for sticking to principles. In either case, those with faith will undoubtedly feel the same as the clowns did as they were herded away by uncomprehending police officers.

> **Deep joy and faith are sometimes not understood by those who do not have them.**

DOING SMALL THINGS

Mother Teresa wrote,

> Do not think it is a waste of time to feed the hungry, to visit and take care of the sick and the dying, to open and receive the unwanted and the homeless, for this is our love of Christ in action. We must not drift away from the humble works because these are the works that nobody will do. It is never too small. We are so small we look at things in a small way. But God, being Almighty, sees everything great. Therefore, even if you write a letter for a blind man or you just go and sit and listen, or you take the mail for somebody—small things—or wash clothes for somebody or clean

the house, you are not wasting your time. Very humble work—that is where you and I must be.[21]

These thoughts of Mother Teresa cast suspicion on the admonition to do "great things for God." This phrase contains a bit too much heroism. Doing great things for God is like letting our light shine before people so that God can get the glory, and us, too, but mostly us. In addition, great things are often too big; we don't know where to start, so we don't. Besides, great things are too abstract; they lure us into replacing concrete action with this abstractness. If our goal is to "reach the world with the Gospel," we are liable simply to keep this goal in our imagination without working it out in reality. The feeling that something is not worth doing unless it is great takes hold of us, and what happens is that we do nothing.

We do, indeed, need dreams and visions. But in view of the fact that we are enjoined to go into our closets and pray secretly, perhaps these dreams should be to do little things.

How can we find such things? We can find them by actively looking for them. We can open our eyes and observe what is in front of us. We can use our inventiveness. Art, technology, and literature demonstrate how inventive we are. Perhaps we can use this inventiveness to discover worthwhile but humble work.

"Simple acts of love and care keep the light of Christ burning" (Mother Teresa).

Simple acts of love and care are the greatest we can perform, but we cannot think of them in that way or they will lose their greatness.

DEALING WITH TEMPTATION

There seems to be little talk about temptation these days, and one gets the impression that no one ever experiences it, but we do. I want to suggest three ways to deal with it.

The first way consists of resisting temptation directly, steeling ourselves against it, fighting our impulses directly. Here it is power against power, desire against desire, that is prominent. To get this power, we might pray or try fervently to keep in mind what we most value or simply say to ourselves, "I don't want that."

This first way certainly does work sometimes. We have resisted strong temptations. However, we have also succumbed. The impulses to pride, malice, avarice, illegitimate sex, envy, spiritual indifference, anger, and gossip are powerful. We know their energy and seductiveness firsthand and we have not always defeated them.

A second way of dealing with temptation is to remove ourselves from situations in which we experience it. This is the principle behind Jesus' admonition to cut off our hands and pluck out our eyes if they cause us to stumble. This way works well for some temptations, such as using drugs or becoming drunk; in these a change of location will often protect us. Other temptations, however, are always with us, such as the temptation to criticize or the temptation to be too proud of our possessions.

A third way is to be captivated by spiritual things. Here we delight in giving love and in being selfless. We wish ardently for the happiness of those in distress and for the transformation of those who have lost their way in life. We want passionately to give companionship to the lonely and to encourage those who are depressed. Søren Kierkegaard aptly characterized this third way when he described the knight of faith as one who has "infinite interest" in spiritual matters.

When we possess ardent wishes, passionate wants, and infinite interest, temptations lose much of their power. They are squeezed out of our lives. Perhaps possessing wishes, wants, and interest is what it means to have spiritual vitality, and perhaps gaining spiritual vitality is the most effective way of dealing with temptation.

> If we never feel tempted, it is either because we are captivated by the divine or because we are enmeshed in the worldly.

"THROW AWAY YOUR EYE"

One of the more puzzling things Jesus says is that if one of our eyes causes us to stumble, we should "tear it out and throw it away." It is better for us "to enter life with one eye than to have two eyes and to be thrown into the hell of fire" (Mt 18:9).

This declaration seems so outlandish that our first reaction is to dismiss it. Surely Jesus could not have really meant it, we say. After all, God made all parts of our bodies, and we should not deliberately harm them. If we took the verse literally, many of us would be without eyes. Certainly that is not acceptable.

Yet this verse expresses one of the significant themes of Jesus' teachings—the overwhelming importance of God's values. So there must be some sense in which Jesus meant the verse to be taken literally. Perhaps this sense can be expressed in this way: If something prevents us from exemplifying what has supreme worth, we should get rid of it. Let us see how this strategy would work for experiencing God's grace.

There are, indeed, impediments to experiencing God's grace. Social status can be one of them. Focusing on social status bases our worth on others' approving our achievements and good qualities, whereas grace bases our worth on God's acceptance of us without regard to our achievements and good qualities. Jesus' declaration is telling us that it is better to give up our striving for esteemed social position, our attempts to obtain a job which others regard highly, and our pursuit of worldly success to possess God's grace than it is to keep these and not possess God's grace. If these prevent us from experiencing God's grace, then, Jesus says, we should cast them out of our lives.

Wealth, too, can be an impediment to experiencing God's grace. It makes us think that our worth is based on what we possess. Jesus is telling us that it is better to give up our wealth, to dump our clothes into a Salvation Army box, to trade in our new cars for old ones, and to set our expensive televisions and CD players out on the curb if these prevent us from experiencing God's grace.

Perhaps an analogy will make plain the literal sense of Jesus' statement. Alcoholics generally cannot resist taking a second drink once they have had a first, and often they cannot resist a first if they are in a situation in which alcohol is present. It is often best for them not to get into situations in which they will be tempted.

Jesus' outlandish declaration is telling us to adopt a similar remedy if we need to. We must remove the source of the trouble. If we do not, we may succumb in an ultimate way, losing what most counts in life.

What keeps us from God either needs to lose its power over us or be cast out.

SPIRITUAL WORK

A life of faith takes a great deal of work, and often this work gets harder as we persevere through our years. I want to mention a number of features of this work.

One of the most obvious is that we must exert effort—effort to develop discipline, to love, and to maintain spiritual sensitivity. For some of us, this feature of the life of faith is the hardest, for often we have only enough energy to get through our daily duties. Getting up spiritual energy frequently is beyond what we can handle or beyond what we want to handle. It is far easier to lie on our couches and imagine that we are loving rather than to make the effort actually to love.

Another feature of working at the life of faith is thinking—thinking about the meaning of virtues and how we can exemplify them, about what the crucial elements of living with faith are, about the direction our lives are taking, about the attitudes and feelings we find in ourselves, about others' feelings and circumstances, in short, about anything that is connected to being a faith-filled person. It is tempting to let anti-thinking forces in our culture—television, entertainment, one-line responses—spill over into our spirituality.

Spiritual work also involves imaginativeness. Living without imaginativeness is likely to be dull and routine, but with it, we become fresh and adventuresome. We seek out new ways to love; we become alert to new opportunities and sensitive to new possibilities. Here, too, social forces—including forces in religious institutions—undercut imaginativeness. It is usually disapproved, or if not overtly disapproved, is not well-received or not openly encouraged. To test this, one simply need ask genuine, but imaginative, questions in institutional contexts, such as committee meetings or Sunday School sessions.

Developing new habits is another feature of working at our faith. Habits can get an iron grip on us, and it is often a great struggle to overthrow old ones and take on new ones.

Still another feature is deepening and broadening our first experiences of grace. It is a mistake to think that grace is just what gets us started on the life of faith and that thereafter our concern is simply with doing things. A central aspect of spiritual work is the extension of grace to every part of our lives so that it becomes an integral element of our consciousness.

A last feature of spiritual work is dealing with emotional issues that we had when we first began our spiritual journey. Everyone comes to faith with baggage inherited from earlier experiences. Some of us have had painful childhood experiences or difficult family situations. What we have to do is work these emotional issues into the new realities of love, joy, peace, and forgiveness.

Spiritual work is usually a bit by bit affair. At times we may make great strides, but most of the time we take little steps. It is important to realize that the latter is okay, for these little steps often represent great effort.

Faith is both passion and work.

HOW CAN WE KNOW OUR VOCATION?

Asking the question "What is my vocation?" does not seem to be as prominent as it once was. It is still a good question, though. I want to suggest three factors to consider in trying to answer it. None of the three is decisive in itself, nor are the three together always decisive. They do, however, point us in certain directions.

The first is interest. God gave us interests, and we can certainly follow them if everything else is equal. It is, in fact, good for us to follow our interests. What kind of life would it be if we had little or no interest in the activity in which we spent nearly half our waking hours?

The second factor is ability. God gave each of us a variety of abilities, so, like the first factor, this one does not tell us what particular occupation to pursue, but like interest, it is good for us to enter vocations in which our best abilities are used. Otherwise, we will feel a certain wastefulness about what we are doing.

The third factor I am going to call "value." By value, I mean, broadly speaking, that our jobs should result in good, both for ourselves and for others. There should be some specific ways in which our jobs enable us to mature, and there should be some concrete ways in which our jobs enable us to serve others. It is important to notice that serving others is not just an attitude—it also involves the content of a job. We may have the attitude that we are serving others in a particular vocation, but it may be that our jobs do not actually produce much real good for people.

Some jobs produce more good than other jobs. In some cases, we can make fairly conclusive judgments about this. In many cases, the judgments are not nearly as certain. Yet we need to ask ourselves, "What difference am I making in other people's lives?"

It should be realized, though, that there is no perfect job so far as this third factor is concerned. We might regard new car salespersons as low on the scale of value because they contribute to the materialist glut in America, but perhaps a college professor contributes to a research and educational glut, causing people to bury themselves in books instead of working actively to help the hungry, unemployed, unloved, and hurting masses in our midst. Even a minister's sermons can subtly and irresistibly tempt listeners to rest content in listening instead of moving people to repent sorrowfully and to love compassionately.

Still, our aim in choosing a vocation should be to make it part of what, overall, we really want to do with our lives. We need to feel a sense of mission in our jobs. For the person of faith, jobs should not just be means of earning money or a way of getting through the week so that we can live on the weekends. The content of our jobs should be as much a part of our life of faith as other more "spiritual" parts.

Unfortunately, we do not always have as much choice as we would like in selecting a job that fulfills these three criteria. We live in a fallen world, which means that social structures do not always present us with opportunities to satisfy our interests, use our best abilities, or serve others. Some jobs deaden God-given creativity, some promote irrelevant luxuries, some contribute actual harm to people, and others have little to do with advancing God's values. Part of the tragedy of human life is that we have to make do with less than ideal situations, but part of the greatness of human life is that we can give ourselves away through our jobs.

> The life of faith is not what we do outside our work, but it is lived through our work.

THE EFFECTS OF JUDGING ON THE JUDGE

The familiar words from the Sermon on the Mount, "Do not judge, so that you may not be judged" (Mt 7:1), state that we are not to judge because we are as guilty as the one whom we would judge, if not of the same fault, of another. There is another reason we should refrain from judging: There are deleterious effects on us when we do. To see what these effects are, we need to see what is involved in judging.

Judging is not the same as simply stating or proclaiming what we think is true; it is not simply stating that we disagree with someone or that we believe that what someone says is wrong. Judging involves having a certain attitude—the attitude of condemnation. We feel that we have to set other people straight, show them that they are wrong and that we are right. We cannot let them have the wrong belief; we have to tell them or someone else that they are wrong.

When we have this attitude, we are less likely to be loving and more likely to say critical things about the person toward whom we have the attitude. It is difficult, perhaps impossible, to be both loving and judgmental at once.

Moreover, when we possess an attitude of condemnation, we expend more energy on others' faults than on our own relation to God. We have only so much energy, and we cannot easily use it for two so disparate activities. In a way, God is saying to us, "What is it to you that they are wrong? Love me."

In addition, a judging attitude obstructs our receptivity to God's grace. Judging is based on a high opinion of ourselves; it solidifies this opinion and enhances our feeling of superiority. These, though, obstruct our openness to God's grace. When we embrace God's grace, we do not feel the need to judge. We do not feel threatened when someone else differs from us.

Unjustified judging hurts the one who judges as much as the one judged.

TWO KINDS OF SOLITUDE

In his wonderful little book *The Way of the Heart*, Henri Nouwen distinguishes two kinds of solitude. Of the first kind, he writes,

> We say to each other that we need some solitude in our lives. What we really are thinking of, however, is a time and a place for ourselves in which we are not bothered by other people, can think our own thoughts, express our own complaints, and do our own thing, whatever it may be.[22]

In this kind of solitude we recoup from stress and busyness, think what we want to think, imagine ourselves doing certain things, and make plans for later activities. We do things by ourselves with no one else distracting us or intruding into our private space. We set aside the demands of work, family, and life itself; we retreat from everyone else. We are, in short, alone with ourselves.

This kind of solitude is good to have, and we need it from time to time, some of us more than others, but it differs from a second kind of solitude, which Nouwen also describes. This second solitude, he says, is "the place of conversion, the place where the old self dies and the new self is born, the place where the emergence of the new man and the new woman occurs."[23]

This solitude is not a retreat, not just something we do for ourselves, not a time of indulging ourselves in our own thoughts. It is, rather, a time in which we ask, in God's presence, the simple question, "How do you want me to change?" Asking this wrenching question about our own transformation, instead of giving us relief from the distractions of life as the first solitude does, increases our inner agitation. It makes us aware of the distressing gap between what we are and what we want to be. It focuses our attention and desire on the latter of these. And it pushes us in directions we vaguely already know we should move in.

We seek solitude for relief, but need it most for change.

NINE

IMAGINATIVE CARING

When Jesus was asked, "Who is my neighbor?"[24] he responded with a story that not only answered this question but also the further question, "How can I love my neighbor?" Perhaps the lawyer who asked the first question really meant to be asking both of them. Perhaps, even, he did not mean to be asking a question at all, but meant to be putting Jesus to a test or defending himself against the charge of not being loving. In any case, Jesus treated the lawyer's utterance as a real question, and he used his response to do more than simply answer the question. He told the lawyer what he could do to love and he admonished him to act as the hero of the story, the Good Samaritan, acted.

The lawyer's question is our question as well. "Who is this neighbor and how can I show her love?" The answer Jesus gives enlarges our conception of love. He tells us that neighbor love consists of imaginative caring. This feature makes neighbor love both more definite and, fascinatingly, more appealing as well.

IDENTIFYING WITH OTHERS' SUFFERING

The central feature of imaginative caring is identifying with another. This feature is especially prominent in the biblical appeal for us to "remember those who are in prison, as though you were in prison with them; those who are being tortured, as though you yourselves were being tortured" (Heb 13:3).

To identify with those who suffer is both to be aware of their condition and feelings, and to have a compassionate attitude toward the condition and feelings. It is not simply being in the same condition or possessing the same feelings, for we may suffer in the same way that someone else does without identifying with that other person. Nor is identifying with others' suffering the same as imagining what we would feel if we were in the other person's position. This is a self-centered attitude that often obstructs our being aware of what the other person is feeling.

Why should we identify with those who suffer? In the first place, such identification is good in itself, for indifference and hardness are bad in themselves. A compassionate attitude is good even if we do not act on it and even if the sufferer does not know we have the attitude. This is especially true in cases where we cannot act compassionately, but it is true also in cases where we can so act but do not (though acting in addition to having the attitude would be much better).

In the second place, it is good for the sufferer to know that we are identifying with her. Our identification is a gift to the sufferer even if it does not relieve the conditions causing the suffering, for it helps the sufferer to bear the pain. The words, "You've suffered," convey our identification. So also do our facial expressions and the looks in our eyes. Active listening does so as well, even though we may say nothing.

Last, identifying with others' suffering can drive us to action. It is, in fact, a potent motivator. It does not always move us, but the more intense it is, the more likely it is to do so.

Perhaps the most effective way to prompt ourselves to identify with those who suffer, and so to act, is to put ourselves in a similar position. We can maintain a subsistence level diet for a time, visit a prison, spend a night on the streets where the homeless congregate, or talk to the involuntary poor. We can also read books and articles about those who suffer, and we can remember times when we have suffered.

In order to be able to identify, though, we need to be transformed. Identifying presupposes an awakening, a turning from a preoccupation with our concerns to those of others. Identifying, in fact, requires something wrenching. The "fat, relentless ego," which we love so well, must be exchanged for self-forgetful attention to another. In letting go of the tight grip our anxieties have on us, we undergo a reversal.

It is also the other way around. In identifying with others' suffering, we become transformed. We become attuned more and more to suffering; we actively look for it so that we can identify with it and be part of its relief, and we suffer as well.

One of the greatest discoveries we can make is that other people have feelings, and one of life's greatest tasks is to identify with those feelings.

BEING MERCIFUL

One of the beatitudes in the Sermon on the Mount says, "Blessed are the merciful, for they will receive mercy" (Mt 5:7).

What does it mean for us to be merciful? It means the same thing that it does for God to be merciful. We accept people even though we know about their faults and even though we find those faults offensive.

The opposite of being merciful is being critical and judgmental. One reason we judge people is that we are insecure. Judging makes us feel superior and consequently more secure. Thus, in order for us to be merciful we need to feel secure, and this comes from knowing—and feeling—that God is merciful to us. When we feel this, we do not need to make ourselves look superior.

The intriguing feature of this beatitude is that our being merciful to people is connected to obtaining mercy from God. It is almost as if we cannot obtain mercy from God unless we are merciful to others. Whether or not this is a theological truth, it seems to be a psychological truth. Our hearts cannot be melted sufficiently to receive God's mercy unless they are melted enough to give mercy to others. Perhaps this is what Ann perceived when she said to me, "I cannot accept the fact that God forgives me until I can forgive my father for what he did to me. And that I cannot do." Her father had raped her repeatedly.

The effect of our being merciful to others is like the effect of God's being merciful to us. God's mercy heals us, and our mercy toward others helps heal them. In each case, being the recipient of mercy has a marvelously restorative effect.

> If we cannot give mercy, we are not likely able to receive it.

COMPASSION

One distinctive feature of being compassionate is identifying with those who hurt. The authors of the book *Compassion* describe this identification poignantly.

> Compassion asks us to go where it hurts, to enter places of pain, to share in brokenness, fear, confusion, and anguish. Compassion challenges us to cry out with those in misery, to mourn with those who are lonely, to weep with those in tears. Compassion requires us to be weak with the weak, vulnerable with the vulnerable, and powerless with the powerless.[25]

There are many ways we can identify with those who hurt. We can feel the anguish of those who are in despair, cry with those who grieve the death of someone near to them, and feel the frustration of those who are involuntarily unemployed. We can eat less for supper and go to bed hungry so that we can experience a little of what Third World peasants experience; we can visit or live in neighborhoods where those who are on the bottom of American society live; we can listen to people who are struggling with personal problems; we can give up our wealth so that we know what it is like to be poor.

Compassion also requires action, but it at least involves the kind of identification embodied in Ivan Denisovich's query, "How can you expect a man who's warm to understand a man who's cold?"[26]

Identifying with those who hurt is not our natural inclination, as the authors of *Compassion* point out.

> Compassion is neither our central concern nor our primary stance in life. What we really desire is to make it in life, to get ahead, to be first, to be different. We want to forge our identities by carving

out for ourselves niches in life where we can maintain a safe distance from others. We do not aspire to suffer with others.[27]

Being compassionate is agonizing for us because we want to make a place for ourselves, feel looked up to, be comfortable, and be respected for our achievements. We also want to feel safe, so we surround ourselves with barriers so that other people will not get too close.

Why is it that these are our motivations? Perhaps it is because we do not feel completely secure. When we do feel secure, we do not have to spend time on activities that produce a false sense of security. We are free to identify with those who hurt. We can be compassionate.

I want to make a plea—a plea to myself but also to those who ardently desire a larger life. It is a simple plea. It is that we give up trying to get ahead and that we identify with those who hurt.

> True compassion requires that we become, in a way, the person who suffers.

LOVING OTHERS

What prevents us from loving others? Perhaps the first answer that occurs to us is that we are too much preoccupied with ourselves. When we focus energy on our own projects and desires, we have little left over for those of other people.

Another answer is that we ourselves may not have been loved, and we cannot love others unless we have been loved.

A third answer is that loving others involves fear of rejection. When we love someone, we take the risk that that person will not be open to our love.

In addition, other people are different from us. They may have a different color or a different social status or be handicapped or look different or wear different clothes or act differently. These differences often work on us unconsciously to prevent us from connecting to them. We may unconsciously think that we are better than they are because of these differences, or feel vaguely that we would lose our status if we associated with them, or simply be afraid to be seen with them.

Insecurity, too, prevents us from loving. We need to feel secure before we can feel safe with others.

A lack of spiritual energy, a lack of "hungering and thirsting" for giving love, also weakens our resolve to love. Most of the time, we have just enough energy to do our tasks, get through the day, and give ourselves a few compensating pleasures for the day's pains. Loving others requires effort above and beyond this survival effort, an effort we often do not have.

Loving is hard work. It is hard to cease being preoccupied with ourselves and to overcome fear of rejection. It is hard to connect with those who are different from us, to surmount our insecurities, and to maintain a selfless desire to be available.

How can we spur ourselves to love? We can set aside our own preoccupations and focus our interest on the concerns of others. We can let ourselves be loved by someone else—a friend, a parent, or God; we can let their love puncture the shells we construct around ourselves. When it does, it will fill us and then spill out almost automatically. We can become aware of our fear of rejection and seek to

overcome it. We can overlook the differences between ourselves and others, accepting them no matter what. We can
work on our insecurities. And we can give ourselves a
desire, a passion, that is not content with the humdrum of
daily existence.

> Everyone has different obstacles to loving, but
> no one is unable to overcome them.

MINISTRY TO EACH OTHER

A common idea in communities of faith is that we need to
minister to those who are destitute, poverty-stricken, or in
trouble. These kinds of people are, indeed, needy, but it is
also just as true that the rest of us are needy.

We need support. We need to be listened to, to be loved,
to know that we are loved, to be encouraged, and to be
praised. We need someone present when we are down,
someone with whom to pray, someone with whom to think
things through, someone with whom to talk about our faith
and our doubts, someone to call us on our birthday, someone to ask how we are feeling, and someone to hear our
confessions. We need to see God in our friends.

These needs are ones we can supply for anyone we know. In doing so, we become ministers to them, not to the neglect of the destitute, the homeless, and the troubled, but as an integral part of our everyday living.

> The more we regard our acquaintances as having deep needs, the more we are likely to minister to them.

IMAGINATIVE CARING

Each of us is extraordinarily inventive. We like to devise new ways to entertain ourselves, new places to go and new clothes to wear. If we are in love, we like to make up new ways to be romantic. Some of us like to come up with new ideas; others like to invent new gadgets. All of us spend a good part of our waking life daydreaming, picturing to ourselves how things might be, and imagining ourselves in different circumstances.

Why not direct our imaginativeness toward caring as well? We can imagine new ways to care—things we can do and words we can say that will convey our caring. We can imagine the attitudes that constitute the caring and the facial expressions that best convey these attitudes.

We can also use our imaginativeness to picture the feelings others have, so that we can identify with those feelings. This way to use our imaginations is, perhaps, at the very core of the caring itself. It is leaving ourselves behind and imaginatively identifying with others. It is self-forgetfully feeling others' pains and joys. This imaginative identification is essential to bearing others' burdens and sharing their delights. We need it if we are to cry when they cry and to skip and twirl when they skip and twirl.

Without imagination, love would die.

GOOD NEWS

It is possible to get news without realizing that it is good news. We might, for example, be walking the trails in a forest preserve, thinking that we know where we are when in fact we do not, and see a sign pointing back to the parking lot. Unless we know we are lost, we would not see the sign as bearing good news. We might be told that a friend is alive, but unless we knew that her life had been in danger, we would not initially react with enthusiasm. In general, we will not be able to recognize news as good unless we feel ourselves to be in some predicament. We will greet such news with a polite "Oh, I see," or even with indifference. But if we recognize that something is amiss, we will welcome news of how to remedy our condition with exuberance and a great sense of discovering our way. Here are some examples:

You wrestle with the feeling that you are not good enough and constantly struggle with a sense of not having worth. Then one evening while you are half reading and half thinking about life, you suddenly realize that God does indeed love you and that you are okay and that you do not have to worry about impressing others. You feel like smiling warmly and genuinely to your coworkers the next day, and you do.

You have done something which causes you shame, or you catch yourself hating someone, besmirching their character behind their backs, and your conscience begins to poke you with sharp jabs. Then, as you are walking by yourself, the thought that God forgives completely and irrevocably comes to mind. Instantly you feel sorrow and aversion and then just as instantaneously, forgiveness, and you continue walking with your conscience no longer poking you.

You have been a victim, hurt by someone you trusted, and you have painful memories. You go long days fighting to survive. Then one day it hits you that Jesus was a victim, too, and that he knows how you feel, because it hurt him to be accused unjustly and then handled roughly as he was led to his execution. You realize that God is a listener and that you can tell him that sometimes you are barely able to live, that you are angry at the person who hurt you, and even angry at God sometimes, knowing that he will still listen to you when you tell him these things. You feel as if someone understands what you went through, and sometimes you smile.

You think of your death, the shortness of life, and you get a knot in your stomach, feel dread and anxiety, and tell yourself that death comes only to other people. Then you remember that God has a new life in store for us after we die, and your dread dissipates, your anxiety melts.

> Scripture is good news, but only to those who know they have lost their way.

WORDS

We often think that talking is different from acting. Our lives consist more in what we do than in what we say, we instinctively think, for it is our actions that define our character, get things done, aid people in distress, and earn money. Talk is cheap, but actions count.

Yet talking is a kind of acting. When we say things, we are, after all, doing something. It is not, to be sure, like the doing involved in working or making something, but it is, nevertheless, an activity.

Moreover, talking occupies a major part of our lives. We spend large quantities of time talking, even if we are the kind of person who is relatively quiet. We cannot easily go for long without saying something to someone. In addition, talking performs a variety of functions. We use it to promise, encourage, forgive, inform, and express, and talking has great power. It moves people to action, breaks up marriages, educates, and prevents catastrophes.

One way words are used is to hurt. The childhood saying, "Sticks and stones can break my bones, but words can never hurt me," is far from the truth. All of us can remember occasions when words have hurt us deeply. Words can be used to express hate and unjustified anger, criticism and rejection. Words can also kill. Those who are depressed may be pushed to suicide by critical words. Continual use of harsh words from a parent may make a child want to run away. "It was not so much what he did, as what he said," an incest victim once remarked about her father.

Words can also be used to love, to care, and to accept. They can be used to heal deep wounds and to save lives. There are numerous times when someone's words dispelled our discouragement. When we have felt guilty, perhaps someone's words brought us forgiveness. On occasion, we may have felt like giving everything up, but someone's words made us feel that life was worth living.

Words can be used to praise, forgive, and to ask for forgiveness. They can be used to lift spirits, relieve loneliness, and dissolve despair. A simple "Thanks" can convey heartfelt gratitude. Words revealing our true feelings can puncture someone else's pretending.

God's words to us are, "I love you" and "I forgive you." These words make us new people; they transform us into something we never imagined we would be.

Many of us are looking for concrete ways of making a difference in others' lives. We may have felt called to become involved in some type of ministry, but not known what kind.

Using words to change people's lives is a lifelong call, one we can start on right away. Yet in another sense it is not one that we can simply do, for we have to become the kind of person who wants to praise, show acceptance, and give encouragement. We must first come to have the desire to give healing words to others. Our personalities must become such that we instinctively regard words as gifts that we delight to give. We also have to engage in creative thinking about the kinds of words that will actually show acceptance and give healing, words that fit our own character as much as the character of the recipient, and we have to become attuned to opportunities in which we can give these gifts.

Using words is as much of an adventure as exploring unknown land, for we rarely know ahead of time what opportunity for using words each new situation will present to us. We hardly ever know how the listener will respond, and often we are not sure we have used the right words. Even so, the adventure is full of surprises that lead us into territory we never knew existed.

> Words fitly spoken restore and rejuvenate;
> so also does quiet, rapt listening.

SEEKING AND GIVING

Most of us have had negative feelings about attending religious services at some time or other. Perhaps we have felt that the sermons were boring or that the people were not very friendly or that the atmosphere was stifling. After getting to know the members of a faith community, we may have felt that they seemed not really to care about true spirituality or that they were hypocritical and uncooperative.

One option we have in such situations is to try to change things in the community. Although this may make us more content, it does not always do so, for we may not succeed in changing everything to our liking. Another option is to find an acceptable community. This, too, may satisfy us, but sooner or later some of the same feelings may recur. We may find that no faith community is just the way we want it to be.

One important thing to realize when we are discontent is that other people may feel about us the same way we feel about them. They may think we are unfriendly, lacking in enthusiasm, hypocritical, stifling, or uncooperative. Yet we would not want them to stop coming because of us.

If we want to make attending religious services part of our lives, then two attitudes are needed: seeking and giving. Seeking—What can I learn about God? What insights into faith can I obtain? Giving—Whom can I encourage? Whom can I help grow in their faith? To whom can I be friendly today? These two attitudes are an essential part of the life of faith. When we infuse them into our life of worship, they give us an entirely new perspective about being in a faith community.

There is always more to find and give.

GOSSIP

It is particularly easy to engage in gossip in tightly connected communities. Churches especially need to be on their guard against it.

The dictionary defines gossip as "groundless rumor." Rumor is defined as "a story current but not authenticated." To these definitions we might add that gossip is not just telling news about another; it is also passing on information that may be harmful to another's reputation.

Gossiping is easy to do for several reasons: It makes us feel superior because it exhibits our knowledge about another person. It also makes us feel superior morally. In displaying another person in a bad light, we are heightened, or so we feel. In addition, when people we are with are gossiping, it is difficult for us to refrain, because the pressure of conformity is so intense. Sometimes we nearly burst with the impulse to pass along something we know.

Gossiping should be avoided for several reasons: First, what we say may not be true. The story we hear may have become distorted by the time it gets to us. Second, what we say may not be the complete story. There may be other information about the person or situation which casts new light onto it and makes it not so bad as it really is. Third, the Golden Rule enjoins us to imagine what we would feel if we were the person about whom we are gossiping. When we imagine this, we instinctively sense the aversion we would feel if we knew someone were gossiping about us. Fourth, gossip harms a person's reputation, and a reputation belongs so intimately to a person that in a sense it is part of her. Last, gossiping hurts us as well, for it solidifies in us a tendency to see the bad in others and to hurt them.

How can we avoid gossiping? First, we need to be sensitive to whether or not facts we know about someone will hurt that person's reputation if we were to tell someone else. We need to differentiate good and neutral information from potentially harmful information. Second, we need to be sensitive to the feelings of people about whom we are talking. We need to imagine ourselves being the person herself and ask how we would feel if someone were to pass on that information. Third, when we are the recipient of gossip, we should not pass it on to anyone else, including our best friend or spouse. This is very hard sometimes, for it means that we must keep some pieces of information concealed for the rest of our lives.

Last, if we are with people who are saying harmful things about someone, we have several options: We can remain silent. We can change the subject as gracefully as we can. We can say something positive about the person. We can say something about not gossiping, such as "I feel uncomfortable talking about her in this way."

With what can gossip be replaced? There are many good topics to talk about. We are inventive creatures and can come up with numerous such subjects. We do not have to have our conversations sprinkled with negative facts about people. One good substitute for gossip is praise of another person. This can be done not only when the person is not present, but directly to the person.

A community that is held together by gossip needs a different kind of glue.

TEN

DEFENDING THE ACCUSED

An outside observer of American Christendom would notice that different segments of it have different crucial tests for being a genuine Christian. The observer would note that many segments have doctrinal tests of various kinds, that some segments have behavioral tests, that others have tests about one's moral beliefs, and that some even have political and cultural tests. She would discover that some of the tests are explicit and publicly stated whereas others are not very explicit or clearly stated.

One's initial reaction to this array of crucial tests is to decry it. Christians should not be setting up tests that divide themselves from each other. If they do insist on proclaiming a public test, it should involve what is crucial to Christianity, not what is non-essential.

With this response in mind, I want to propose what may seem like another test. It is, "To what extent am I willing to associate with people who are on the bottom of society, with those who are neglected and scorned because they do not fit in, and with people whom others won't have anything to do with?" I do not mean for this to be a public test, but I do mean it to be a crucial question that people of faith need to ask. This is because faith itself is tied to our willingness to connect with others regardless of their social status.

THE FINAL JUDGMENT SCENE

One of the most vivid and striking narratives of Jesus is the final judgment scene in Matthew 25. There are two prominent features of the portrayal. The first is that our obtaining eternal life is said to depend on what we do, and the second is that the kinds of things we are to do involve those who are on the bottom of society.

Jesus says,

> Then the king will say to those at his right hand, "Come, you that are blessed by my Father, inherit the kingdom prepared for you from the foundation of the world; for I was hungry and you gave me food, I was thirsty and you gave me something to drink, I was a stranger and you welcomed me, I was naked and you gave me clothing, I was sick and you took care of me, I was in prison and you visited me" (Mt 25:34-36).

Those who receive eternal life are those who have aided "the least of these who are members of my family"—the social rejects, the poor, the ill-dressed, the chronically unemployed, the criminals.

This passage is puzzling, for it seems to say that our ultimate destiny depends on the actions we do or do not perform instead of on faith, as other passages in the Bible say. How can our salvation depend on doing things if it is a matter of faith in God's saving mercy?

The answer is that we cannot possess faith in God's saving mercy unless we have humility, and we cannot have humility unless we are willing to associate with those who are in the lowest strata of society. This humility is "humbling ourselves." It involves not trusting our social position and successes as the source of our security. It means setting aside the conception of ourselves as good because we are not poor, ill-dressed, unemployed, or criminal.

Deep within us resides an intense need to feel good about ourselves. We have an almost intoxicating desire to get this feeling from other people—from their approval of us, from the fact that we are better than they are in specific ways or higher than they are on the social scale. Though we do not consciously say to ourselves, "I thank you, God, that I am not like that unkempt homeless person who just walked past me," we nevertheless feel this at an unconscious level.

If we get our sense of self-worth solely from other people, we will not be able to associate with the rejects of society. To do so would be to lower ourselves, to make ourselves vulnerable to the disapproving glances of others. It would be to risk our self-worth, which is based on the disassociation of ourselves from unsuccessful people, people with whom we do not want any association. It would be like a corporate business executive exchanging crisp, smart clothes for frayed cuffs, scrubby shoes, and an ill-fitting dress or patched pants. Can we imagine anyone doing this?

Those who have taken in God's unconditional love, however, acquire their sense of self-worth from God's acceptance of them. They do not risk their self-worth when they associate with those below them on the social scale. They can be with them without worrying about the condescending attitudes of others for doing so.

If all this is so, then the judgment scene in Matthew 25 is extraordinarily revealing, not only of God's intent and of what is required to have saving faith, but of the basic motivation of human nature. It says that we must change our fundamental drives and demonstrate that we have done so if we are to make it into eternity.

A faith that is not at least willing to associate with those at the bottom of society may be no faith at all.

AN UNSEIZED OPPORTUNITY

Some years ago, some of the faculty members of the college where I teach were flown to Miami to celebrate the incorporation of a school in Miami into our college. We were told not to walk anywhere alone because the downtown area where we were staying contained a large number of homeless people and a high crime rate. I had also heard that there was a shantytown nearby. Being curious, I went exploring to see if I could find it. After wandering around for awhile, I finally found it under an eight lane highway overpass, between two city streets. As I approached it, a young man came out of it and said "Hello" to me. I was a bit startled, but returned his greeting and struck up a conversation. He asked if I would like to be shown around. I responded that I would, so we went in.

The shantytown consisted of about fifty shacks made out of cardboard, scrap wood, metal, and other debris. Generally, they were no larger than seven by ten feet or taller than six or seven feet. Some were smaller and a few were larger. Many had some kind of chair beside them and many also had a cooking apparatus—a beat up grill in some cases and a fire on the ground in other cases. All of the residents were African-Americans, most were men, and a few were children.

My guide introduced me to a number of the residents. I shook their hands sometimes; other times I simply greeted them and talked with them briefly. Some were very friendly; others were somewhat wary; one person eyed my back pants pocket where my wallet was and started to pull me into a shack. I resisted and we went on our way.

During the course of my visit, which took no longer than twenty or thirty minutes, my guide became more and more enthusiastic and amazed at my being there. "This is a work of the Holy Spirit," he exclaimed several times. I had not been beaten or robbed. The people in the shantytown had received me cordially.

From the shantytown we went to other locations where the homeless stayed. They had staked out areas under the overhangs of buildings and set out their beds and a few belongings. My guide showed me his own place, an area about five by eight feet with another eight or so similar areas all in a line under an overhang on what appeared to be an unused shelter in a park.

During our time together my guide was telling me about himself. His wife and two children were staying somewhere else. He had contact with them often, but was unable to find enough work to keep them all together. I came to trust him. I began to think about giving him some money when we parted. I had in my wallet two one dollar bills and a twenty dollar bill, no change, and no other bills.

The time came for us to part. We had been together about an hour and a half. Both of us had felt moved. He asked me if I could spare anything. I reached into my pocket and gave him my two one dollar bills. He accepted them graciously, and we went our ways.

That day I missed an opportunity to give Jesus a twenty dollar bill. I had given my guide my address with the intention of sending him more money if he had written. But he never did.

> Seized opportunities account for a large share of the way we love.

MUGGING THE VULNERABLE

In a recent experiment, videos were made of people walking along crowded city sidewalks. The videos were then shown to prison inmates, who were asked to identify the people they would most likely mug if they could. Interestingly enough, there was a great deal of unanimity in their selections. Even more interesting was the fact that a group of psychologists who had been asked to identify the people in the videos who were most defenseless and vulnerable made the very same selections that the professional muggers had made.

This ingenious experiment confirms what is evident anyway, namely, that it is the vulnerable who are most likely to be taken advantage of. They are more likely to have their rights violated, to have undue power exercised over them, and to be influenced in illegitimate ways. Because they cannot stand up for themselves, others are tempted to do things to them that they would not otherwise do.

Everyone is vulnerable in some respect or other, but there are people who are more vulnerable than others. The poor and the uneducated, for example, are easily taken advantage of. So are the senile, the handicapped, the very young, and the economically dependent.

God has a special concern for the vulnerable. Scattered throughout scripture are statements that exhibit his care for the weak and defenseless. Amos, for instance, denounced the people of Israel for trampling the poor and for depriving them of justice in the courts. Jesus, in his inaugural speech in the synagogue, stated that he had been anointed to preach good news to the poor, to proclaim freedom for prisoners and recovery of sight for the blind, and to release the oppressed. And James said that pure and genuine religion is to take care of orphans and widows in their suffering.[28]

The word from God is that we should treat people without regard to their status. This means several things: It means that we ought not to mistreat those who, for whatever reason, are weak and vulnerable. It also means that we should not give special treatment to people who are at the opposite end of the scale—those who are financially secure and educated, for example. Their needs and rights should be respected, not because they are financially secure and educated, but because they are people. Finally, it means that we should come to the defense of those who are easily taken advantage of. We need to stand up for them, because they cannot do it for themselves.

Tertullian wrote, "It is our care for the helpless, our practice of loving-kindness, that brands us in the eyes of many of our opponents."

People who are mugged, whether by professional thieves, twisted justice, oppressive economic structures, or unequal opportunities, are likely to be helpless. What would it be like if society branded people of faith as ones who care for the helpless?

> **Professional muggers are not the only ones who can easily identify the vulnerable; those with an enlivened faith can as well.**

ON SEEING WHAT IS RIGHT IN FRONT OF US

Selective perception is a well-known psychological phenomenon: We see what we want to see and do not see what we do not want to see. In different words, our conceptual mindsets cause us to focus on some of what we see and to ignore other parts. For example, we interpret ambiguous drawings in different ways, depending upon what inhabits our minds at the moment of seeing.

An example of what may be selective perception in the Bible is the story of Lazarus and the rich man (Lk 16:19-31). The rich man dressed in purple and fine linen and feasted sumptuously every day. Lazarus, however, lay at the gate of the rich man's estate. He was covered with sores and was so hungry he pictured himself crawling under the rich man's table, picking up and devouring the droppings. No doubt the rich man passed by Lazarus many times. It may be that he saw Lazarus and deliberately refrained from aiding him, but it is also possible that he passed Lazarus without really seeing him—he didn't want to know about his troubles. Perhaps in a certain sense the rich man did not know Lazarus was sitting in front of his house.

There are conditions that we, too, may not know about due to selective perception. We may not know about involuntary poverty or discriminatory treatment of those who are different from us racially, even though these conditions are there for the seeing. We may not observe depression or loneliness in our friends, even though clues are prominent. These examples show that selective perception is also a spiritual phenomenon. We do not want to become mixed up in something that is alien to us, so we tune it out.

How can we see what is right in front of us?

We can come to possess a passion for seeing. This involves wanting to see what is going on, wanting to know what others are feeling, and wanting to be aware of pain, trouble, and distress.

We can put ourselves into circumstances in which we cannot help seeing what is happening. Isolation insulates, but being with someone who hurts forces us to listen. This remedy for selective perception requires some boldness.

We can develop perceptiveness: noticing facial expressions and tones of voice that reveal depression, observing social conditions that suggest racism or affluentism. This remedy requires some subtlety.

We can increase our inquisitiveness. The superficial "Hi" reveals little, but interested questions open up a box of surprises, as do probing, reading, and thinking. This remedy requires curiosity.

Of these four ways of opening our eyes, the first may be the most significant. It is akin to the hungering and thirsting for righteousness mentioned by Jesus in the Sermon on the Mount (Mt 5:6), the seeking first of the kingdom of God (Mt 6:33), and the spiritual fervor of the apostle Paul.

Many of the people we encounter are Lazaruses.

LISTENING TO SERMONS, READING THE
BIBLE, AND LOOKING FOR AN ANXIOUS FACE

It is a manifest, but significant, fact that Sunday morning church services nearly always contain homilies or sermons. Eliminating them for more than a Sunday or two would be a departure from a long and well-established tradition. Not only would the church hierarchy have something to say about the missing sermons, churchgoers would as well. In some traditions, the paradigm of good Sunday morning church participation is the rapt sermon-listener taking notes and studiously referring to biblical passages that are mentioned by the minister.

Sermons are important because they address the content of faith. However, there is a caution one must exercise with respect to them, a danger against which one must be on guard. Because they deal with content, they can be sources of evasion. Listeners can focus so much on content that they become numbed to the emotive aspects of faith—sorrow for pain, remorse for shortfalls, gratitude for love, delight in magnificence and moral beauty.

The same is true of reading the Bible. Although it is true that the ardent believer cannot refrain from reading it for long without feeling empty, it is just as true that reading it can obstruct our relationship with God. We can center our attention so much on what we read that everything else that is important in the life of faith gets eclipsed.

Kierkegaard once suggested that if reading the Bible prevents us from connecting with God, we should gather our Bibles, pile them up, and set fire to the pile. Some of us may need to do this. We may be so Bibled-up or full of sermons that we need to abstain for a time—not to get away from faith, but to rejuvenate it. We may need to start listening to suffering humanity, deliberately putting ourselves into positions where we cannot fail to notice the pains and joys of others. We may need to set aside our usual habits, which have become lifeless and mechanical, and pray the tax collector's prayer. Instead of taking in a sermon, we may need to look for an anxious face.

Religious exercises both enliven and deaden.

LIBERATION

When we think of the main themes of the Bible, becoming free comes to mind. God is said to free us from the grip sin has on us. Paul declares that the wages of sin is death, but that the free gift of God is eternal life (Rom 6:23). Through faith we are offered rejuvenation and freedom from destructive habits and ways of acting.

The Bible also speaks of other kinds of liberation. One of the central events of the Old Testament, the Exodus, involved liberation from political and social oppression. If we were peasant farmers living under a repressive government, black people living in South Africa, or women in Afghanistan, we would identify with the Israelites and would think of God as a liberator in more than just an individual sense.

Throughout the Old Testament, God is said to have a special concern for those who are under a heavy weight: God desires justice for the fatherless, the widow, and the oppressed; he loves the sojourner; he remembers prisoners, the blind, and those who are bowed down.

In his first temple speech, Jesus mentioned several kinds of underdogs. "The Spirit of the Lord is upon me, because he has anointed me to bring good news to the poor. He has sent me to proclaim release to the captives and recovery of sight to the blind, to let the oppressed go free, to proclaim the year of the Lord's favor" (Lk 4:18-19). The remarkable feature of this pronouncement is that Jesus is claiming to be a liberator to those who are burdened socially and physically. The good news he has is directed to those who are oppressed in these ways.

In Paul's great Galatian declaration of equality, he writes, "There is no longer Jew or Greek, there is no longer slave or free, there is no longer male and female; for all of you are one in Christ Jesus" (Gal 3:28). These are social and political categories. Paul is telling us that God frees us from unjust inequality.

It is easy to miss these other kinds of liberation. Those of us who are supposedly "on top"—white, affluent, male, free, American—have a good deal to lose from God's liberation. We, therefore, tend to run right past these troublesome passages in scripture, or we spiritualize them to blunt their sting. Then, too, we belong to an individualist culture, so we tend to see religious matters only in individualist ways. As a result, we read into the Bible what we want to see in it and miss the God who is really there.

Liberation is, indeed, individual—salvation is liberation from our own sin. God deals with us as individuals; he can scarcely do otherwise. But liberation is also corporate—God liberates us as a people from other kinds of bondage as well.

> Freedom for those on top turns into oppression unless it is accompanied by freedom for those on the bottom.

RACIAL RECONCILIATION

One of the social inequalities that Paul's affirmation of equality speaks to is racial discrimination. To the Jew and Greek, slave and free, male and female—categories that oneness in Christ abolishes—we might add black and white, Mexican and North American, Native American and mainstream American. Paul's declaration means several things:

It means, first, that racial reconciliation should be a personal and political priority. Racial reconciliation should matter to us, and we should make ourselves aware of it. We should not simply be indifferent to it or avoid thinking of it. We should study the political issues involved with race, vote for candidates who make it a priority, join political organizations that give it as much importance as they do other issues, and become "white supremacist watchers" so

that we can defend the rights of their victims and participate in counter-demonstrations.

It means, second, that we should take the initiative. If
racial reconciliation is high on our agenda, we won't just
wait until someone else does something about it. We will
do things on our own. We will take risks, just as we take
risks for other issues that matter to us. We won't say, "I
haven't hurt anyone of a different race." The plain fact is
that animosity between races exists, and where it does not,
uneasiness does.

Taking the initiative means that we will ask those of
other races about the issue. The situation is like that in
which friends have come to have hard feelings between
each other. One option in such a circumstance is simply not
to say anything and hope the feelings go away. Sometimes
this may be the best way. Often, though, one of the friends
must raise the subject in order to restore the friendship, difficult as it may be to do so.

Paul's affirmation means, third, that we will notice
ways in which racial interaction takes place. We will be
aware of how we are acting toward someone else of a different race. We will probe our attitudes. We will become
aware of income disparity, housing patterns, and other
forms of subtle segregation.

Racial harmony needs to be worked at or it
will disappear.

WHAT IF WE WERE IN PRISON?

The Golden Rule enjoins us to do to others as we would have them do to us. One way to exemplify this is to imagine ourselves being someone else and to ask ourselves how we would feel if we were in their circumstance. Suppose, for example, we were to imagine ourselves in prison. What would we feel?

Perhaps the first thing we would feel is shame. We would be reluctant to see our friends and would not be able to look them in the eye when they visited us. We might try to convince them that we are innocent or explain away our misdeed in some other way, because we would not be sure that they would still like us if they believed we were guilty. We would want them to show that they still accept us.

If we were not guilty of the charge against us, we would feel that an injustice had been done to us, and the longer we stayed in prison the more intense our feelings would become. They probably would be directed to the "system," about which we might become disillusioned. If we had been sentenced to death even though we were innocent, we would be enormously frustrated and heartbroken when people did not believe in our innocence.

We would be annoyed at some of the prison rules. We would not like it when prison authorities took down pictures we had put on our cell walls on the grounds that they were fire hazards. We would feel oppressed at not being able to make more than two ten-minute phone calls a month—when the phones were working. We would be humiliated at the strip searches required to go outside to the "yard," and would probably forego the trips in order to avoid them.

The constant noise would drive us crazy. Our nerves would be racked due to the inability to get more than five or six hours of sleep at a time because of the high noise level. We would be exceedingly frustrated at not getting even ten minutes of solitude, unless we had been placed in "the hole," in which case the solitude would make us listless and numb.

We would agonize over moral dilemmas presented by prison life. When we discovered who had beaten another prisoner, we would want to tell the prison authorities, but would be afraid to do so for fear of retaliation. We would be tempted to join a gang so as to get protection from physical harm. We would dread sexual assault.

We would be lonely beyond words and would long for letters and visits from friends and relatives. We would want to read, but would be frustrated at having little access to decent books. We would get enormously depressed at times, and if we were on death row would feel overwhelming gloom. Perhaps we would yell and scream at indiscriminate times, at no one in particular, in order to vent our emotions.

We would feel that even though we were in prison, we were still a person with worth, and would want others—prisoners, guards, and acquaintances outside—to feel the same way and not to treat us as scum. We would feel that we still have basic rights, rights to proper medical attention, respect, and protection from physical harm.

Last, we would feel that no matter what we had done, we were not beyond being loved by those on the outside, and we would be starved for it.

To imagine ourselves feeling what others feel is sometimes enchanting and sometimes wrenching.

DEFENDING THE ACCUSED

After going through the closing transaction for the purchase of our first house, my wife and I talked with our lawyer about his job. "What I like to do," he said, "is to defend people who have been unjustly accused." I was surprised at this, not because I thought it unusual that a lawyer would want to defend the accused, but because I thought then that this is what all lawyers liked to do.

The lawyer's remark prompted me to ask what role defending the accused should play in the life of the church. Should it be a peripheral role, an optional activity which would be nice to do but which the church could get along without? Should it be a more central role, something we would expect believers to do and be surprised if they did not? If we broaden the range of the accused beyond those who have been unjustly charged with doing something wrong, then the answer, I believe, is that defending the accused should be a central task of communities of faith.

The accused include those who have been unjustly discriminated against because of their skin color, nationality, sex, or age. It includes those who have been taken advantage of because they are vulnerable in some way, those who are relatively helpless because of personal, social, or economic circumstances. It includes those who lose their jobs and cannot find new ones, victims of crime, sexual assault, family battering, or governmental torture. Among the accused are the poor, the elderly, the unborn, the ugly, and the scorned.

Does the Bible say anything about these kinds of people? I ask this as a real question, because if we are not among the accused we are likely to overlook references to them. What we find is not just an occasional reference to the accused, but repeated references. These references often portray defending the accused as the essence of spirituality and not just as something extra.

In the Old Testament, God gave to the Israelites a number of instructions regarding treatment of the poor. For example, the Israelites were told not to pick their fields clean at harvest time, so that the poor could come and take what they needed. In one of the most revolutionary passages in the entire Bible, the Israelites were instructed to return their property to its original owner every fifty years, so that those who had lost out during that time could have a new opportunity to regain what they had lost.

Isaiah, one of the great prophets, depicts God as castigating Israel for going through the motions of being religious without having true spirituality. What is this spirituality? "Is not this the fast that I choose: to loose the bonds of injustice, to undo the thongs of the yoke, to let the oppressed go free, and to break every yoke? Is it not to share your bread with the hungry, and bring the homeless poor into your house; when you see the naked, to cover them, and not to hide yourself from your own kin?" (Is 58:6-7). True fasting, Isaiah says, involves rescuing the oppressed, not just refraining from eating and cultivating a worshipful attitude toward God.

Amos pleads, "Let justice roll down like waters, and righteousness like an everflowing stream" (Am 5:24). The context shows that Amos is not talking about law and order or punishment for criminals, but about equality of opportunity for those at the bottom of society.

The first time Jesus gave a talk in the synagogue, he stated that he had been anointed to preach good news to the poor, to proclaim freedom for prisoners and recovery of sight for the blind, and to release the oppressed (Lk 4:16-21). James writes, "Religion that is pure and undefiled before God, the Father, is this: to care for orphans and widows in their distress, and to keep oneself unstained by the world" (Jas 1:27). In both of these places, the accused are given a prominent position.

These passages indicate that a central aim of the Christian church should be to help those who are unable to help themselves, love the unlovely, defend the unjustly accused, aid victims, create work opportunities for the poor, and care for outcasts.

It should be admitted straightaway that doing these things is not very appealing to those who are not poor, outcast, or victimized. These activities are not glamorous and they involve people whom most of society regards as having lesser value. It is more exciting to adulate heroes, and it is more comfortable to work on our personal attitudes (under the guise of being spiritual) instead of associating with unattractive and sometimes smelly people.

What would the church be like if it were the kind of institution that was known to work on behalf of the accused?

Spirituality that concerns itself only with one's own growth, good as it may be, is one-sided.

NOTES

1. Blaise Pascal, *Pensees*, trans. A. J. Krailsheimer (Pengiun Books, 1966), p. 323 (#941).

2. Psalm 42:1; see also Matthew 5:6.

3. Søren Kierkegaard, "Every Good and Perfect Gift Is From Above," *Eighteen Upbuilding Discourses*, trans. Howard V. Hong and Edna H. Hong (Princeton University Press, 1990), p. 44.

4. Leo Tolstoy, *The Death of Ivan Ilyich*, trans. Lynn Solotaroff (Banton Books, 1981).

5. See also Luke 12:15.

6. Nicholas Wolterstorff, *Until Justice and Peace Embrace* (Eerdmans Publishing Company, 1983), p. 158.

7. Frederick Douglass, *Narrative of the Life of Frederick Douglass, an American Slave* (Doubleday and Co., 1963).

8. Baruch Spinoza, *Ethics in Works of Spinoza*, Vol. II (Dover Publications, 1951), p. 271.

9. Augustine, *Confessions*, trans. John K. Ryan (Image Books, 1960), p. 43 (Book I, Ch. 1).

10. See Psalms 130:1, 142:3, 142:4.

11. Iris Murdoch, *The Sovereignity of Good Over Other Concepts* (Cambridge University Press, 1967) in Robert B. Kruschwitz and Robert C. Roberts, eds., *The Virtues: Contemporary Essays on Moral Character* (Wadsworth Publishing Company, 1987), p. 87.

12. Pascal, *Pensees*, p. 64 (#131).

13. Carl Jung, *Psychological Reflections: A New Anthology of His Writings, 1905-1961* (Princeton University Press, 1973).

14. Søren Kierkegaard, *Practice in Christianity*, trans. Howard B. Hong and Edna H. Hong (Princeton University Press, 1991), pp. 16-19.

15. Alan Jones, *Exploring Spiritual Direction: An Essay on Christian Friendship* (Harper and Row, 1982), pp. 6-7.

16. Malcolm France, *The Paradox of Guilt: A Christian Study of the Relief of Self-Hatred* (Hodder and Stoughton, 1967), pp. 19-20.

17. Søren Kierkegaard, *Works of Love*, trans. Howard and Edna Hong (Harper and Row, 1962), pp. 277-278.

18. Søren Kierkegaard, *Concluding Unscientific Postscript* in Robert Bretall, ed., *A Kierkegaard Anthology* (The Modern Library, 1946), p. 234.

19. Brother Lawrence, *The Practice of the Presence of God* (Fleming H. Revell Company, 1958), p. 13.

20. Sister Maura Eichner, *Walking on Water* (Newman Press, 1972), p. 70.

21. Mother Teresa, *Life in the Spirit*.

22. Henri Nouwen, *The Way of the Heart* (Ballantine Books, 1981), p. 14.

23. Nouwen, p. 15.

24. The parable of the Good Samaritan, Lk 10:29-37.

25. Donald P. McNeill, Douglass A. Morrison, Henri J. M. Nouwen, *Compassion: A Reflection on the Christian Life* (Image Books, 1983), p. 4.

26. Alexander Solzhenitsyn, *One Day in the Life of Ivan Denisovich* (Time, Inc., 1963), p. 34.

27. *Compassion*, p. 6.

28. Amos 5 and 6, Luke 4:16-21, James 1:27.

A professor of philosophy at Trinity College in Deerfield, Illinois, Clifford Williams is a graduate of Wheaton College with a Ph.D. from Indiana University. In *Why Aren't We Satisfied?* Williams offers nearly one hundred meditations to assist the reader to develop a deeper spiritual life.